Front Cover

This photograph is typical of the kind of meeting of [illegible] ould occasionally take place somewhere in the wilds [illegible] am fourth (counting the baby) from the left with n[illegible] sie standing behind me. My mother is to the left of [illegible] of Jessie. I cannot recall ever playing with another E[illegible] around my own age so the little fellow next to me must have been q[illegible] a novelty – his mum and her baby to the left of my mother. The sturdy African to the right stands smartly in a military 'At Ease' stance – possibly ex Tanganyika Rifles and general retainer of our friends.

To Keith

With Our Love

 David & Rosemary

ISBN 978-0-9927570-1-4

19/4/21

Dedicated to
Jesus Christ my Lord and Saviour
and
Rosemary my wife

Acknowledgements

Firstly, in checking several drafts as writing progressed, I have been hugely grateful, in my dyslexia, by my proof readers, Jean Brown, my darling wife Rosemary, Joanna Will, Imogen Thomas and Mathew Backholer. Final editing was completed by Mark Porthouse who has also been my continual source of IT support towards the possibility of publishing these reminiscences.

As author of this book, I, David Dare, take full responsibility for its contents.

Introduction

Once upon a time, just before "the winds of change" dissolved the mighty British Empire, a young British colonial man could still have a wonderful time wandering through parts of Africa. Such was my good fortune. In writing this autobiography, I have been saved from self indulgence by including the many times I have been blessed by the generosity of others and the number of extraordinary people I have met along the way. I have also been privileged in experiencing the radical events and developments that have occurred during my eighty two years – politically, socially and in communications technology.

Table of Contents

1. Introduction

A tribute to my parents

My life has always been influenced by the extraordinary example of my parents' nigh on fifty years of service with the Salvation Army. That began in the 1890s for my mother in Scotland and my father in Essex. Their full-time service began during the 1914-18 war. They then led Salvation Army fellowships in England for ten years before their pioneering service in Tanganyika between 1934 and 1944. It was during this period that my mother thought she had malaria aged 45 in 1938, but it was actually me!

Before their retirement to the UK in 1958, their crowning achievement was in training Officers to lead the Salvation Army throughout East Africa in later years.

The following photographs are of them shortly before their retirement and of one of their Nairobi Training College sessions.

I am most grateful for being born into my Christian family as well as for many personal and business related friendships. My personal pilgrimage in faith 'took off' halfway through my life and greatly impacted on subsequent events. I momentarily plunge some forty years ahead to halfway through my story with the following drama to illustrate that Christians have an obligation to share the Gospel of Christ notwithstanding discouragements against doing so.

Idi Amin and the death of my close friend Paul Lennox

In 1960s Uganda, I experienced the danger of having anything to do with the infamous President Idi Amin, who was associated with the death of my close friend Paul Lennox. That would be some forty years ahead of me writing this memoir. I soon realised that telling others the Gospel of Christ could involve spiritual opposition but, at the same time, it could be 'underwritten' by God's promise in Isaiah 55 that "His word will not return void." Under the heading "Full circle and pause for reflection" at the end of this book, I record how this principle has held true throughout my Christian life.

During a stopover in Nairobi en-route to the Seychelles in the mid 1970s, I was entertained to supper by charter pilot Paul Lennox (pictured right) and his wife Sheila during which I shared my testimony of having accepted Christ as my Saviour and Lord. Paul dropped me off at my hotel, at which point we paused as I asked Paul where he stood spiritually. Of all my friends, Paul was a man of exceptional integrity so I was not surprised when he said he wanted to make his peace with God. He declined my offer to lead him in prayer and he simply prayed for forgiveness and invited Christ into his life as Saviour and Lord.

Shortly after this, Paul was hired to fly two businessmen to Entebbe, Uganda to meet President Amin with Paul not realising that they were military arms dealers. While Paul's aircraft was parked at Entebbe airport, rival arms dealers placed an altitude bomb in Paul's plane which exploded as Paul descended to land back at Nairobi killing Paul and his passengers. Sheila phoned me with this awful news and I returned to Nairobi to pay tribute to Paul at his funeral and share Paul's recent surrender to Christ and my personal assurance that he was safe with God.

Bizarrely, around 1959, Idi Amin, still a sergeant at that time, was invited by his British commanding officer at Jinja Barracks, Uganda, to occasionally play rugby for our Nile Rugby team when I was also playing for that team.

The Gospel of Luke 23v39-43 describes how one of the two criminals crucified with Jesus feared God and said “Jesus remember me when you come into your kingdom” Jesus answered him “I tell you the truth, today you will be with me in paradise.” How wonderful that we can be assured that my friend Paul met his Saviour before he died.

Now, after that digression, I can proceed with this book.

These reminiscences were typed during two 2020 COVID-19 ‘Lockdowns’. Years previously, I wrote short, anecdotal homilies. I have included some of these in this autobiography as well as a few black and white photographs and pencil sketches.

A kaleidoscope

A kaleidoscope was both a favourite toy of my childhood but also a wonderful metaphor for my future life. It comprised a small tube like a telescope, containing bits of coloured glass and plastic reflected by mirrors so that various symmetrical patterns appeared when the tube was rotated. The patterns of brilliant colours constantly changed as one turned or shook the tube. Similarly, my life has been enriched by wonderful people of different races, tribes and nationalities. I have been blessed through seeing landscapes and wildlife, homes, skies and seas of beauty beyond description. It would, however, take a while for me to make the connection between all this and the Psalmist’s observation:

"The heavens declare the glory of God; the skies proclaim the work of his hands." Psalm 19v1.

2. 1938-54: Childhood and Schooldays

Parents Frank and Jessie Dare
First World War, Belgium 1916
Salvation Army Ambulance
and Canteen Services

Tabora, Tanzania, 1941
Sister Jessie, 18
Brother John, 11
Me – aged 2

On 28th April 1938, I was born under two flags. Firstly, picture our British 'Union Jack' with me, combining the crosses of our three countries England, Wales, Scotland.

Then try to visualise the red, yellow and blue Salvation Army flag; red for the blood of Christ (forgiveness and cleansing from sin); yellow for the Holy Spirit and blue for holiness. Central to the flag is its motto "Blood and Fire", again standing for the blood of Christ and the Holy Spirit.

Four years before I was born, early on Easter morning 1934, the Union Flag hung from the flag pole outside the government offices in Tabora, Tanganyika – now Tanzania. The Salvation Army flag flew proudly at the head of the very first 'Army' march through the town. Bleary-eyed Africans, Indians and Arabs watched Officers Frank and Jessie Dare marching towards a mango tree at the centre of the town. A single African – Salvation Army officer Madete, beat a big drum. Frank played a concertina and sang a hymn with his wife and Madete while the children carried their father's cornet and concertina cases. The African officer announced the purpose of their arrival – to proclaim the Gospel of Jesus Christ.

Like the founder of the Salvation Army, General William Booth, they began "driven on through every sort of hardship and discouragement – by the love of God and by a passion to save lost souls." They would continue to do so throughout the following eleven years. They were brave in the face of opposition from Islamic Arabs who lived with them in Tabora which was located on the old slave road to the coast. Most testing of all – greater than endemic malaria, wild animals and poisonous snakes – must have been the feeling of isolation from loved ones at home. Letters could take three months to turn around during the Second World War and that conflict prevented them from taking any home leave for eleven years, during which both lost their parents. Oh, and then they had to send their two very young children off to boarding school.

An African village in the bush at night

I had contracted Cerebral Malaria aged two. That disease is described as "involving parasite-filled blood cells that can block small blood vessels to the brain, causing brain swelling and possibly brain damage." Apparently, malarial parasites were to blame in my case. All I can remember was appalling head aches. That was apparently accompanied by a dangerously mounting body temperature. Miraculously, my life was saved by a young British medical locum who injected quinine into my spine.

This illness left me with a peculiar mixture of legacies. One was my inability to learn to read, do sums or make any sense of colours or written music, despite the dedicated efforts of my sixteen-year-old sister Jessie. I eventually read my first word unassisted – "FORGET-ME-NOTS" at the age of seven. Even so, I have crystal clear recollections of ordinary life scenes from my very early childhood. The other main legacy was an insecure spirit probably caused by our family move from rural Africa to bomb-blitzed England in 1944 when I was six. Now – that African village in the bush:

It was the practice of my missionary parents to explore areas in Tanganyika which they had not visited before. It must have been on one of those journeys that we arrived at a small African village in the bush after sundown. I remember the beauty of smoke from a wood fire veiling the scene of scantily-clothed villagers standing around the fire in the centre of a few very basic African huts. Secondly, I remember the scent of the smoke itself emanating from tropical firewood. High above in the unpolluted sky were the stars. I still identify with the description of God's creation in the book of Job in the bible: "while morning stars sang together and all the angels shouted for joy" (Job chapter 38v7). My tiny heart shared some of that joy.

Before proceeding further with these reminiscences, they will occasionally refer to instances when I was to find myself faced with a situation or challenge for which I lacked the essential experience and/or intellectual capacity to cope. At that point I will record that something remarkable happened or, miraculously, this or that happened for me to complete the task.

1944: The Noah's Ark scene

The year is 1944. At the bottom of the Nairobi escarpment in Kenya, my father stopped his old 1934 Chevrolet. I was 6 years old and both of us were astonished at the picture we beheld. We had stopped because a huge number of animals, herd upon herd, had begun to cross the road below us.

There were buffalo, impala, giraffe, zebra, wildebeest and various other antelopes. I suppose that we must have stood still for a quarter of an hour, so great was the number of animals. As a child I was familiar with the story of Noah's Ark and certainly, in front of us, we seemed to be seeing a repeat of the scriptures. I think that this was a kind of epiphany for me.

Curiously, I was to have a second experience of this sort years later in almost the exact same spot. I was alone, motoring in the other direction, and had been stopped by a puncture. I had been motoring through the night from Uganda and, as I put on my spare wheel, I realised the sun was coming up. Slowly, light was advancing down the side of the Rift Valley, gradually dispersing the darkness as the sun advanced. Later I was to read from the book of Ecclesiastes in the Bible how "God has made everything beautiful in its time" (chapter 3v11). Strange that, even now, I can remember the tingle of admiration on this occasion and years earlier, with my father.

I remember another beautiful scene during the rainy season which sometimes necessitated putting our car on a flat rail carriage to avoid impassable mud. One moonlit night, one of my earliest memories was waking during such a journey and watching the moonlit savannah and acacia trees drifting by with just the 'clickity-clack, clickity-clack' sound as we passed slowly over the rails beneath us.

During visits to South Africa (in the 2010s), we met Bishop Eric Pike and his wife Joyce of the Anglican Church of South Africa. Eric has encouraged me to take an interest in the Christianity of the Celts of the 4th to 9th centuries after Christ. The Celts pointed to the beauty of our origins in God and not to the superficial differences of race, language and culture. They held that "sin has distorted but not erased the deepest image of the beauty of our origins in God." I have personally found that these insights of the beauty of our origins to be a refreshing balance against an emphasis that can tend towards understanding that what is deepest in us is our sinfulness. My parents seemed able to rejoice in finding that the beauty of our origins in God was 'nearer the surface' of the hearts of their new African neighbours, than they might, initially, have expected.

Interestingly, Dad would not have known it at the time, but he was on the threshold of training sufficient indigenous Army Officers to lead hundreds of Salvation Army fellowships throughout Kenya, Uganda and Tanganyika. We would soon sail to the UK for Dad to take up a two-year assignment after which my parents would pour all their past experience into being joint Principals of the Officer Training College at Nairobi in Kenya.

My ashtray memento

The ashtray is beautifully crafted from the base of a large, brass, discharged military shell. The following words are inscribed on its underside:

To David from his Italian prisoner of war friend Deo, Tabora 1944.

This gift was presented to me by an Italian prisoner of war at the camp situated just over the road from our house at Tabora. Because of its distant location from civilisation – five hundred miles of bush separated it from the coast – the prisoners were allowed regular exeats. Passing by, my friend would tell me of how he missed his own son in Italy. My mother would sit us down for a chat and cup of tea in our garden. I have a photo of Deo and I enjoying our unusual friendship – like two old men outside a cafe in Rome!

Dad launches his ministry

John and I enjoy our cricket with Jessie keeping wicket and dad bowling

Two unwelcome guests while Dad was away on safari

I enjoy tea with Deo my Italian detention camp friend

Then in late 1944, we start my parents' first home leave. I, in my shorts, learn to shovel snow away from one of our numerous accommodations while my parents tell various Salvation Army corps all about their pioneering work in Tanganyika.

A well for the blind camp

Our family befriended a number of these Italians, some of whom helped my parents with jobs like tuning our piano and fixing my father's car. We also received valuable assistance from them related to a camp for blind Africans which my father was building ten miles from Tabora on a plot granted by the government. Unfortunately there was no water there. My father happened to mention this to the Commandant of the camp who said, "I have just the man to help you." My father soon took this Italian 'water diviner' to the camp. He spoke no English but on arrival got out of the car, went into the bush and selected a large fork from a tree shaped like a chicken wishbone.

The man grasped the ends of the long parts of the fork holding its apex upwards. He spread it apart and proceeded to walk up and down the centre of the plot. Suddenly, the apex forced itself towards the ground. The man stood still at that point and proclaimed, “Isa water here!” My father, with some scepticism had some workmen dig a well at the spot and, sure enough, water was found seeping onto a flat rock eighteen feet down. More help was provided from the prisoner’s camp whose bricklayers beautifully lined the walls of the well and installed a hand-pump which supplied the blind residents for years afterwards.

My father appointed a wonderful African officer named Ndamu to manage the blind camp. Ndamu also introduced the residents’ guests to the Gospel of Christ no doubt including Christ’s own words in John 4v17 when Jesus said, “Everyone who drinks this water will be thirsty again, but whoever drinks the water I give him will never thirst. Indeed, the water I give him will become in him a spring of water welling up to eternal life.”

My father arranged for an intelligent blind boy to be trained as a telephone operator. Years later, that young man was on duty at the Tanzanian international telephone exchange in Dar-es-Salaam when my father was calling from England and needed to be put through to Tabora. The young man recognised Dad’s voice! Later still, when I was in Tabora doing field research for FEBA radio, I spoke to an elderly Muslim emerging from a mosque who enquired how I knew the local language. When he heard that I had been born there and that my father had been the founder of the Salvation Army work there, he proved that he remembered my Dad in typical, African style. He said, “Your father walked like this,” and limped off a few steps as my father did with his club foot. That same Muslim man turned out to be grandfather of the telephone operator and expressed his appreciation for the help his family had received from my father. Small world!

1936-1938: We nearly lose my brother John

It was 1936 – 2 years before I was born. My parents got an emergency call from John's boarding school to say that he was seriously ill. My parents motored overnight and arrived at the school in Arusha just after the surgeon had operated on John. He had appendicitis and also hookworm. My mother stayed for a number of weeks to nurse him and eventually he pulled through but didn't fully recover until he was in his teens.

"Missionary-speak" in those days included a phrase describing some sacrifice that circumstances forced upon them – such as having to send children off to boarding school. They stated that they were being forced to put it, or their children, "on the altar". It may sound quaint but, for the children involved, the damage could last a lifetime. Certainly, John had nightmares about that schooling well into his adulthood.

Rescue for John came in 1944 when we moved to the UK. At school there, he shared a desk with a lad whose brother ran a gymnasium. He introduced John to weight training which transformed John during the 2 years we were in the UK into a more extrovert personality with lots of charm and a fine physique. Personally, I owe him a great deal for his friendship. He looked after my interests as a young boy when my parents were heavily occupied with their missionary work and my older sister had married and departed.

My childhood memories of John relate to his boarding school holidays. He was extremely inventive at making something out of very little. I remember him building a large kite. Once, when there was a steady wind, he sent it aloft and tied the string to a tree so that the kite simply hovered up there until he lowered it. On another occasion he carved a tiny model of a yacht from a piece of wood and I watched him sail it on the town's small reservoir.

How did my parents do it?

I would like to reflect on that anecdote about brother John and his kite being held up by the wind. What wind? Tabora was hot and dry with hardly a breeze except, presumably, when the rains came. How, I ask myself, did my astonishing parents, with less than the proverbial shoe string, maintain their sanity, helping poor lepers, prisoners or Africans who were actually blind, or blinded by witchcraft. How did they and my sister Jessie, who helped them, keep going? Then it has dawned on me.

In Ephesians 3v14-21 the Bible speaks three times of "the power of God's love". The wind holding them up – illustrated by John's kite – was surely the power of the Holy Spirit of God and His love working in and through them throughout, not just their eleven years marooned at Tabora, but throughout their fifty or so years serving with the Salvation Army. They had met in the First World War battlefields, my father an ambulance driver and my mother in the Salvation Army 'Red Shield' canteens offering a cup of tea during the soldiers' – perhaps last – hour off from the ghastly trenches. That must be the only answer – they were filled with the power of God's Holy Spirit and Love as were the Apostles we read of in the book of Acts in the Bible. What an act for my brother John and myself to follow!

Perhaps their greatest encouragement came in seeing the transformation they saw in the lives of their flock. This resulted from my parents ‘walking the walk of Christ’ as well as the new life God breathed into these people through hearing Christ’s good news of forgiveness, purpose and eternal hope.

The cleanest ostrich in Africa

Before leaving our time at Tabora, I must write of the “Cleanest Ostrich in Africa”. My mother was puzzled by the large quantity of blue soap bars being used by her laundry assistant. Then, my father watched a neighbour’s pet ostrich taking an interest in our laundryman. When he moved away to hang out clothes to dry round the corner of the house, the huge bird sneaked over and pinched the soap which my father saw slipping down its long neck. Mystery solved.

We all move on from our childhoods and so must I with these reminiscences.

1944: Sailing to the UK

Early in 1944, my parents received notice that, at last, passage for our family was booked on a ship from Mombasa to the UK. The Phelps family, farmers at Arusha, had cared for Jessie and John on their school exeats. They now said we should wait for our sailing date using their cottage at Malindi some distance from Mombasa on the Indian Ocean coast. The shape of the Malindi bay in those days channelled the sea waves to impressive heights and I always remember the sound of those waves at night, crashing onto the beach in front of the bungalow. I say "in those days" because those 1940s waves later receded a quarter of a mile out to sea. This was because, after political independence in 1962, the bay began to fill with billions of tons of earth eroded from up-country due to de-forestation for firewood. This ruined the waterfront hotel business.

Into World War Two

I reflect on this stark change as a metaphor for the equally violent transition from my childhood to the war still raging in the UK. During our passage at sea, musical Jessie and John had entertained passengers on deck with their guitars and voices in harmony, but come the Bay of Biscay – quite another story. Our little ten-thousand ton steamer rolled and tottered between mountainous waves and my father and John had to take their turn on Deck Watch against German navy ships. Our dining tables were fitted with frames to stop our meals from falling into our laps. We were eventually welcomed into the Thames estuary with the sound of air-raid sirens, search lights, the sound of detonating bombs, fire and smoke. My childhood innocence was at an end.

Aunt Maud's staircase

My father's sister, dear Aunt Maud, came to our rescue that first night at Southend. There, I remember her gentle kindness, her garden apple trees and the voice of Bing Crosby on the wireless!

In her home, there was a steep staircase between the bedrooms and the bathroom/loo. One night, during the enforced blackout, Jessie turned right too early and sleepily tumbled down the stairs sustaining a few minor bruises. I told her that she was a silly girl and did exactly the same thing a few nights later! With Jessie about to marry her Rhodesian fiancé and depart and leave us, I would soon learn to play the guitar and sing with John, memorising all sorts of western and romantic ballads which were inappropriate for my boyhood mentality.

The first UK tour around relatives and churches then return to Africa

During my Missionary parents' Home Furloughs over the years, they were allowed a few weeks of holiday then had to tell various churches about their overseas work. Fortunately, as we travelled sympathetic and mature male cousins would have me join their usual free time activities but one soon felt that we were overstaying our welcome. I itched to return to Africa. The war officially ended soon after our arrival but food rationing continued for some time, then there was the 1947 coldest winter on record and London disappeared under fog generated from coal fires.

Little circuses and fairs reopened in Essex where we returned again to Aunt Maud from Scotland. Loud speakers often played "The bells are ringing for me and my girl" for returning servicemen and I managed a few months at a school in Thundersly, Essex. I could not cope with my first school in Scotland. It was the first time I was shut into a dark, claustrophobic room, so I escaped and ran home (shades of things to come).

Treats with Dad

On two wonderful occasions, I had my warm-hearted father all to myself. He took just the two of us to a cafe for tea and we were each able to choose a cake from a display cabinet. One other treat in his company was listening to the prize-winning Black Dyke Mills Brass Band in a London park. I can now imagine that he might have been thinking, “I used to be bandmaster of a band like that.”

I never managed to establish that sort of relationship with my mother. Due perhaps, to her extremely hard childhood, she seemed distant, and that might have caused me to hesitate about marriage for a long time. On reflection, my behaviour towards young ladies was generally cavalier and I greatly regret that I must have caused sadness among some. Certainly it all contributed to exaggerated, emotional peaks and troughs in my later life.

My mother, like Catherine Booth, wife of the Army’s founder, was “Mother of the Salvation Army” and a huge support to my father throughout their lives and wherever they served. I mention just one example of her loving industry on behalf of the local people. It involves an intake of one hundred Salvation Army officer trainees – fifty couples – when my parents became the Nairobi College Principals in 1947. Thirty of the fifty couples had very young babies. My mother had thirty cots made from discarded wooden pallets. She also collected machine-sewn nappies and sheeting that European friends had sewn out of surplus bed linen. The mothers were taught to daily wash the linen and scrub the cots leaving everything to dry in the sun before morning classes. At 5.00am each morning, my mother personally supervised the cooking of African maize porridge for all one hundred students.

1947: Happy days at Parklands Prep School

At last, father was appointed Salvation Army Officer Training Principal in Nairobi. Phew, what a relief. The College was in Eastleigh, an Indian suburb of Nairobi. From there, I was able to cycle to my happy days at Parkland Junior School where the headmaster Mr Brindley and all the teachers were wonderful. There I chummed up with Mick Bennett who remains my great friend until now. We currently Skype monthly between George, South Africa and Lyme Regis, England. Mick had been adopted by his most wonderful grandmother 'AMB' who served a delicious oxtail supper on Fridays! In the school holidays, I played Indian games with youngsters of our Indian neighbours and we flew kites carrying lanterns at night during their Diwali festivals. Big brother John would sometimes take me on safari with him and we occasionally stayed in the most wonderful, colonial homes of his friends out in the country.

I have to smile about minor irritations that occurred between us Parklands school boys and boys of another, local junior school. I was being threatened by one of them outside the Westland shops when his mother came by. She saw what was happening and to ease relationships, invited me to his birthday party the following Saturday. I much enjoyed her baking and the differences between us faded away after that!

An angel saves me from drowning

There were no pools where I could learn to swim as a boy so I had no sense of danger when we went on our first holiday by the sea at Malindi. Close by was the beautiful Blue Lagoon with brightly-coloured corals which lay close to the beach.

It was low tide as I wandered into deepening water with the tide coming in. My elder brother John was bandaged up with treatment for boils and was sitting under a palm tree some distance from me when he heard my plaintive cries for help.

The coral I was standing on had taken a sudden dip and I was bobbing up and down with my arms in the air. John raced down the beach, into the water and fished me out. I was choking with water and fright but safe. In retrospect, the salt water might have helped cure John – I hope, but seriously, I would surely have drowned had it not been for my fleet-footed brother.

The Prestons

The Prestons were to me, among the most remarkable Kenya pioneer families. I had contact with them as a boy through their grandson Billy. Roland Preston had been trained by the Indian Railways as a foreman plate-layer and was in charge of the rail laying gangs building the main Kenya railway between 1897 and 1903. Living in a tent, he was accompanied all the way from Mombasa to Lake Victoria by his indomitable wife Florence through adventures like attacks by the man-eating lions at Tsavo who devoured many of the Indian labourers and delayed progress for some time.

I met his grandson, Billy Young, at school in Nairobi. We sometimes sat at Roland's feet when he was very old and huddled in a chair with a hot-water bottle on his lap, telling stories of his years building the railway. Roland's son, Vic Preston was a hero of mine because he pioneered motor sport in East Africa, personally racing motor cycles and cars. I was within earshot of Vic in the 1940s when he and friends initiated a car rally around Kenya to celebrate our Queen

Elizabeth's coronation. That subsequently became the famous, regular, international, East African Safari Rally.

In contemplating eight further periods of my life and at this point in my writings, I received complimentary comments from a trusted friend who read these early reminiscences. I replied as follows:

"Thank you for your encouragement. I never had a book in mind – perhaps a few sketches that might somehow encourage others. In praying before re-starting, I was reminded of Psalm 45v1, 'My heart is stirred by a noble theme as I recite my verses for the king; *my tongue is the pen of a skilful writer.*' I thought – that's it – let me prayerfully let the Holy Spirit be co-author of these reminiscences. Only recently have I realised how I have been the beneficiary of God's 'Everlasting Arms' beneath me over the years (Deuteronomy 33v27), mostly unrecognised and unappreciated. With this fact now in mind, I proceed with the hope of sharing other experiences that might interest, entertain and, in some way, encourage others.

1952: Prince of Wales secondary school, Nairobi

In 1951, I followed brother John into the Nairobi European Secondary School, The Prince of Wales, as a boarding student. In the very first class, one had to call out one's full name. Because my mother was born in David Livingstone's birthplace and he being a missionary, I was christened David Livingstone Dare. I was henceforth called Livingstone by a few of the boys.

A tough walk: The story of David Livingstone, Explorer

Between 1841 and 1872, the Scottish, missionary-explorer Doctor David Livingstone, walked over 20,000 miles in central and south Africa. For several reasons, he is my travel hero.

As a disciple of Christ, he consistently practised his master's patience with trying people and difficult circumstances. Like Christ, he set captives free.

During this period, the slave trade was rampant. Dr Livingstone's geographical discoveries gave him access to large audiences during his rare visits home to the UK. He publicised the suffering and death which he had seen Arab slavers inflict upon Africans. They suffered as they were marched to the coast for sale, then packed into ships for cruel voyages into slavery.

Dr Livingstone also suffered from perpetual malarial fever and from the greed of the African chiefs whose territory he had to cross. They demanded gifts from the trading goods which he needed to continue his campaign. His left arm was permanently injured by a lion attack. He was often cut off from news of his family. During one continuous period, he never saw another white person for five years.

During these 30 years in Africa, his strength came from reading his Bible and his faith in God and his mission. He patiently continued to do good and believed that all would work out well in the end. Most of the Africans he met had never heard the good news of Jesus Christ. He told them this Gospel and treated them from his scant store of medicines. At one stage, all his supplies were generously restored by the journalist Henry Stanley. On several occasions, his stores were plundered.

He earned such respect that his life was saved on more than one occasion by the very Arabs whose trade he was to destroy. When he eventually died in central Africa, some of his porters carried his remains between 900 and 1,000 dangerous miles to the coast. There, the British Navy took him home where his doctor identified the damaged arm bone.

Dr Livingstone was laid to rest in Westminster Abbey and it was not long before effective steps were taken against the slave trade.

1947 blissful move to Kenya and Parklands Primary School for me

One holiday, brother John takes me on one of his Caltex Oil safaris

In 1952 I move up to Prince of Wales Secondary School. There I have two very supportive friends throughout four years – Mick Bennett a day student (Stinker) like me who lived across the road from the school, and John Plough a boarder from Mombasa – photos taken much later.

On leaving the PoW school, I worked for Frank Howitt on his goldmine at Busia on the Kenya Uganda border. One Christmas, several of the Howitt family gathered there and Frank's sister Dulcie took care of the catering for all of us.

A year later, I accepted a lift to Salisbury, S. Rhodesia to visit my sister Jessie and family.

Entering the Prince of Wales School, I immediately and without explanation, experienced an emotional trough and meltdown. I could not cope with the claustrophobia of dormitory and tight time schedules and soon had to convert to being one of the one hundred day students or “Stinkers” as we were described by the ‘superior’ five hundred boarders. My chum Mick Bennett was also a day boy as he lived just opposite the school which helped. Initially, I cycled seven miles each way from Eastleigh until my parents relocated nearer the school.

Life was also brightened by boarder John Plough of Mombasa who was in the same ‘B’ stream class as me. He also became a lifelong friend and only recently passed away in Canada.

Mick’s grandfather J. Bennett traded ex-military kit among which were large box-kites designed to raise aerial wires for military signals. In our spare time, these were great fun and almost lifted Mick and I off our feet as they rose and then the kites dived if we slackened our strings. John Plough and I spent endless hours playing ‘gaining ground’ – kicking a rugby ball to out distance each other up and down a field.

The Prince of Wales headmaster Philip Fletcher and all the teachers were inspiring. They and the friendship of my two chums enabled me to enjoy reasonable progress in lessons and sport. The four years there were punctuated by holidays during which I escaped our Salvation Army College home into local holiday jobs in Nairobi or, in his generosity, brother John let me join him on some of his business trips.

3. 1955-58: Last 'Colonial days', Gold Mining; Farming; National Service

Pals who were always good for a laugh

Brother John had two friends, Brian and Sid whose home was in Mombasa on the coast. John and Brian teased Sid about his tiny old Austin Seven car. Sid bet them £10 that he could drive it the three hundred miles to Nairobi. They agreed. Sid set off and was confronted by an elephant as he drove through Tsavo. Sid reversed but exited the car and climbed a tree as the approaching elephant gained on him.

When the elephant touched the hot radiator cap it screeched and flattened the poor little car. John and Brian let Sid off the bet after Sid hitched his way back to Mombasa with the radiator cap as a memento.

Brother John's other friends and their grand homes

John worked for Caltex Oil Co as a salesman. Over my years at PoW School, John covered sales areas in Uganda and Tanganyika as well as Kenya. Travelling with him, I saw areas of all three territories. History was to repeat itself when I also worked for Caltex from 1958 to 1966. In his good company, I early aspired to having a company car and a salesman's freedom. More of that later except one anecdote about our visiting John's Italian friends, the Rocco family who farmed near Naivasha. John had been at school with their son.

I was enchanted by the contrast of the magnificence of this home and the bush/farmland in which it sat at the edge of Lake Naivasha. To mention just one of its features, the lounge ceiling was two stories high with marble-furnished bedrooms looking down from balconies onto the lounge. Oh, and their two daughters continually played a record of Tino Rossi singing "J'ATTENDRAI"! I guess I was twelve at the time. I still regularly play a CD of that song.

In mentioning Italian friends, Kenya was also awash with Greek sisal farmers (producing rope fibre) and British settler farmers, some famous for developing farm crops and animals resistant to tropical diseases. Indians galore came firstly to help build the railways then to stay on to develop commerce. Afrikaners came from South Africa to teach European farmer-settlers how to train oxen to clear virgin land then plough it for every type of agricultural crop. There was also a sprinkling of many other nationalities who came to share in the opportunities of beautiful East Africa. One must not forget the British colonial Government and Police officials. Often highly qualified, they provided their abilities, mostly on very humble terms of service, to help build these nations.

Wind the clock forward some thirty years, Rosemary and I paid a visit to the Rocco home. It was being tenanted by a U.N. charity and was very run down. An

Australian charity worker welcomed us by displaying an exquisite sculpture she had found overgrown in the nearby bush. It was of a dachshund with its forelegs on the shoulders of a weeping child comforting her by licking away her tears. Then I remembered that the late Mrs Rocco had been an artist and sculptor.

1956: Gold-mining in Uganda then military training in Southern Rhodesia

After school and still only 17, I was at an awkward age, awaiting national service call-up into the Kenya Regiment to fight the Mau Mau uprising in Kenya. Brother John's friend Frank Howitt was reopening an old goldmine on the Kenya/Uganda border at Busia. He offered me a job supervising the recycling of old mining waste while he subcontracted for the Public Works Department clearing bush for a new, adjacent road to Jinja. On the mine, we converted the previously, poorly processed earth into a slurry and washed it over a copper plate covered with mercury which trapped any gold. We separated the mercury and gold in a small furnace and took little ingots of gold into the local bank at Tororo. At the time, it fetched £14 an ounce compared to the present day £1000 per ounce.

Never a dull moment on the mine

Standing over three feet tall with a six foot wingspan, beautiful Kavirondo crested cranes usually mate for life but for a while, we were adopted by one of their number at the Busia gold mine. It may have been attracted by food at the nearby stream and the pool by our house.

We enjoyed its tame presence in two particular respects. It would perch on our roof at night and give a warning call if anything untoward came onto our compound. Each morning, it would daintily step into our dining room when we were at breakfast to accept a share of our toast. Surprisingly, our dogs accepted its stay until we were sorry to see it fly off never to return.

Frank and Dulcie were walking along bush paths around the mine one evening when the dogs ran ahead. Presently, one rushed back in an excited state. They turned a bend to find the other dog being suffocated and completely encircled in the coils of a large python. Frank unhooked its tail 'anchor' from one end of the dog and handed it to reluctant Dulcie. He then tore the snake's mouth away from the other end of the dog. Between them, they wrestled the dog free, uncoiling the snake after which Frank crushed the snake's head with a rock. Easier said than done.

We were about to seal an abandoned, flooded mine shaft. One of our dogs chased a trespassing village goat which fell thirty feet down the shaft followed by the dog. They were both floundering in the water so I had our workmen lower me on a rope to rescue the dog and they helped the villager recover his goat. We then sealed the shaft.

One Friday afternoon, Frank's Caterpillar tractor burst a main hydraulic pipe. He was working to a tight contract clearing bush for a new road. He sent me off that evening in our old Peugeot 203 'light lorry' to get a replacement pipe 250 miles away in Nairobi before the agency there closed at midday Saturday. The main road was being rebuilt and I had to traverse a long and muddy detour via Kisumu overnight. I got to the agency just in time then went to my parents' Nairobi home to rest, asking my mother to wake me in the evening. She saw my exhaustion and let me sleep on until I woke at noon on the Sunday.

I needed another night's rest to recover before the long drive back. Frank recognised he had asked too much of his teenage assistant and appreciated receiving his spare part even though he had lost a day of his contract.

In clearing the bush my employer worked in tandem with an Afrikaner, Public Works Department (PWD), sub-contractor called Hugo who was laying tarmac. One day, Hugo asked if I would sleep a night in his caravan down at his camp as he had to attend a function elsewhere. I could, he said use a camp-bed under a mosquito net. I said I didn't want to use his caravan. As it happened, I could not fulfil that arrangement because a problem arose at the mine. On his return, Hugo reported that lion paw marks were found where the camp-bed would have been and that his dog was missing. This is just one of several occasions when my life was spared during my eighty-two years.

The Southern Rhodesian Regiment

After a year I was offered a lift with some Afrikaners down to Southern Rhodesia to see my sister Jessie and her husband Ken and their family. There I took a clerical job in the Salisbury office of Caltex Rhodesia until I found myself called into the Rhodesian Regiment for a period of infantry training. No one anticipated what was soon to follow in S. Rhodesia. Ex RAF hero, Ian Smith would declare

"Unilateral Independence" from British rule. This was then followed by the Mugabe-led black rebellion against Smith's local white rule.

During military training, I was regularly criticised for my marching on parade. Then, one night, when I was walking between barracks, a security light behind me showed that my natural walk was like that of a sailor, swaying from left to right. This meant my rifle bayonet would sway while those of all the other men held steady. I soon learned to hold myself steady on the march.

I had an attack of malaria, was admitted to the camp sanatorium and was surprised to find myself in a ward reserved for officers. Come meal times, I had fruit salad and ice cream while the lads in the main ward had rice pudding. All rather a mystery until, on being discharged from the 'san', I was called to a halt by the commanding officer of the camp who enquired what regiment my father was in. Then the penny dropped. On entering the camp, I had to register my next of kin and mine was Brigadier F.G. Dare. That was an extremely senior military rank which had obviously caught this officer's attention. I explained that my Dad was in the Salvation Army. This commanding officer smiled, chuckled and walked away without comment. I did not care because I had already enjoyed my ice cream and fruit salad.

Having inadvertently avoided the Kenya war against the Mau Mau, providence was about to have me avoid the awful violence of the Rhodesian uprising when I worked on Rhodesian farms before returning to post-Mau Mau, peaceful Kenya.

1957-58: Farming in Southern Rhodesia

While at the Heany baracks in Bulawayo, I chummed up with a farmer's son Binks Philips, who invited me to visit his family. In doing so after the army, his father offered me a job on their tobacco and maize farm in The Mvukwes, north-west of Salisbury. The notion of producing tobacco did not repel me at the time especially as it was Rhodesia's main cash crop. I was graciously treated as a member of the family for several months before hail wiped out their crop and Mr Philips could not afford to retain my services.

Virginia tobacco seeds were so tiny that a farmer would carry sufficient for a whole crop in his coat pocket. One would put a teaspoon of these into a watering can of water, stir it round then pour it steadily along a prepared seedbed. In a few days that bed would be packed with plants to be transplanted four feet apart in the lands. The plants grew up to four feet high with large leaves. The bottom leaves ripened yellow first and were the first to be reaped and cured in squash-court sized buildings. Then came the tedious process of grading the leaves for the sales floor in Salisbury, according to colour and blemishes. I used to play local radio music to the African staff during their grading. This was 1957/8 when I first heard and loved Belafonte and his calypsos – "Island in the Sun" etc.

I preferred tall maize crops with their foot long cobs. We would tour the lands of an evening after planting. After a few days there was nothing to see, then suddenly, one morning, they were all four inches tall. These lovely plants came under attack from wild pig when the cobs began to form. They would use a tusk to plough down a whole row then eat the cobs. We would use a spot-light to shoot these pigs at night and furnish our tables with delicious pork.

One day I was hitching a neglected , old five-disc plough to a tractor. No matter what adjustments I made, it would go off at a tangent. An elderly farm hand asked me to hand him the spanners and he had it ploughing nice and straight first time. Another time, I was assisted by one of our native farmhands Thomas, to resurrect a damaged combine harvester. He was a tall, fatherly, pleasant fellow who became a real friend. I sometimes wonder what became of him and the thousands of farm employees who were displaced when Mugabe's thugs violently removed the white farmers and asset-stripped their farms.

As I write, I break off for my monthly Skype chat with Mick Bennett, my oldest friend in South Africa. Sadly, violence is endemic there too, not just black against white farmers who provide the main 'bread basket' for the nation, but even more so, indigenous blacks attacking Africans from countries to the north. These illegal immigrants come south seeking employment because the economies in their own countries have imploded, apparently due to government corruption. Magnificent Africa, so full of natural resources, but lacking leadership integrity – so sad.

For a short time, I earned my keep on a remarkable farm owned by the Salvation Army in the Mazoe Valley near Salisbury and managed by an ex-farmer from the west country in the UK. Major Lewis had me running overhead power lines from a generator on the river to the farm buildings. After this, I obtained the position of Maintenance Assistant on a farm managed by Howard and Val Garmany who became great friends. There I enjoyed resurrecting vandalised equipment.

I am introduced to the music of Paganini

Allow me one anecdote before I departed that farm. It involved my introduction to the classical music of Paganini. One evening, after I had farm workmen burning firebreaks and sending them home, I was about to mount the farm motorcycle when I heard violin and orchestral music coming from beyond a large copjie (rocky hill) outside our boundary. I followed a track in that direction and beheld an extraordinary mansion perched high up another copjie from which the music was emanating through a kind of front drawbridge! I followed a winding drive up to the house and was greeted by a tall young Dutchman named Vanstalk. He was managing that tobacco farm, living in the mansion which contained a huge, ten speaker radiogram. We became friends and enjoyed listening to music together – including Paganini's Violin Concerto No. 4 in D minor. The violinist was Arthur Grumiaux. I proudly possess an LP of this exact performance which I recently found in a Lyme Regis charity shop.

Easter 1958: The memorable drive back to Kenya – 1,000 miles without a windscreen

After a year at the farm, I received news from my parents saying they were shortly to leave Kenya for retirement in the UK. How was I, without savings or car, to urgently visit them 1,500 miles back up the Great North Road?

'Providence' again intervened in a truly remarkable way. I phoned the A.A. office in Salisbury who said, "We have a lady here at this minute needing someone to drive her and her dog in her VW Beetle to Nairobi over the forthcoming 1958

Easter weekend." My employers appreciated my situation but I was sad to leave them.

This journey deserves a paragraph of its own. I had not realised how much I had missed Kenya and friends during my three year sojourn in S. Rhodesia. The terrain was mostly flat compared to the Kenya Highlands. Shortly after leaving Salisbury, our windscreen was broken by a stone thrown up by a truck coming in the other direction. We were unable to get it replaced until we reached Arusha in northern Tanganyika three days later. Along the way, we were amused by a parrot stationed outside the loo of a wayside Inn. It kept repeating "Feeling Better?"

I did however have one regret on leaving Rhodesia. I had left the three farming families who treated me so kindly without a backward glance or subsequent letter of thanks. I suspect that I somehow allowed the hospitality and provision our missionary family received in my youth, to develop an unpleasant and selfish attitude that the world somehow owed me. This also applied to the lovely Irish family, the McCrackens in Salisbury, who accommodated me in their 'granny-flat' when I first arrived there from Kenya. At least, I learned to pray for them as individuals over the subsequent years.

As we crossed the borders first into northern Rhodesia then Tanganyika, I felt elated as we got closer to the Kenya border and 'home'. Good old brother John was awaiting our return on Easter Monday evening at the famous Norfolk Hotel in Nairobi. He and his wife Patricia introduced me to their first child, two year old daughter Michele. They kindly accommodated me until Caltex Oil Co took me on as a Salesman, undoubtedly influenced by John's good performance and my father's Salvation Army reputation in East Africa. I was soon able to visit Mombasa and see my parents off to the UK.

A re-union with my old friend Mick Bennett came as I first visited central Nairobi. He was in company with Babette from France who soon became his wife. Soon after meeting Mick, I bumped into the mother of John Thorne, another friend from junior school days at Parklands. John had married a lovely young lady called Helene who produced twins – a boy and girl.

4. 1958-1965: Caltex (East Africa) Ltd on returning from Rhodesia

Dictionary definition of 'halcyon days': "period of peace and happiness" well describes the years following my return to East Africa from S. Rhodesia.

Firstly, I digress about 'Home Leaves': It was really strange how, in my life, history was about to repeat itself. Instead of lengthy periods between missionary visits to the UK, I now encountered the quaint three yearly Home Leaves for some European overseas business employees. One presumed this was to help them recover from tropical rigours. Actually, life in the highlands of Kenya was bliss and not bad either in Uganda or Tanganyika. The pattern for me was to fit parents into however else I wanted to spend the time (I disliked) in the UK. That was shortened by using the option to spend some weeks at sea going or returning. One had the choice of flying one way and sailing the other. I was to encounter poignant situations during two of these leaves.

1959: Uganda – The great writer of business letters

My first boss in Caltex was Duncan McLeod in their Uganda, Kampala office. After warmly welcoming me, he asked whether I knew how to write a business letter. Being the bumptious twenty year old I answered in the affirmative even though I had done no written work for the previous three years. Duncan handed me a typewriter and paper and instructed me to write to an imaginary business addressee on a simple matter and left me to it. I stumbled through the keys and brashly laid my offering before him. He examined my letter and said "David, you do NOT know how to write a business letter!" He remained my boss for the next two years. Not only did he personally demonstrate how one should courteously conduct oneself in business, but he and his wife Rowena kept open house for me when I came into town from travelling my designated sales area throughout eastern Uganda.

When the time came for my first 'home' leave to the UK, I took my parents on a coach-tour through the countries where they had served the Salvation Army in WW1, mainly Belgium via France and Switzerland. Dad's club foot saved him from serving in the trenches. Instead, he drove Salvation Army ambulances and my mother served in Salvation Army Canteens near the trenches. That is where they met around 1916.

Sister Jessie (left) & husband Ken Durman were my anchor home during my three years in S. Rhodesia

in 1958, I returned to Kenya to see my parents, here in my beloved MG, off to their UK retirement

Dr Peter Williams at Arua, Uganda. Peter was recipient of one of three petrol tanks Caltex donated. Long after, he said he had prayed fourteen years for my conversion to Christ

The Kenya Sikh community provided this gracious, white-bearded gentleman to rent and operate our Caltex service station close to Government house, Nairobi

Old Bill Holmes incredibly became a millionaire when he kept N. Rhodesian copper mines supplied with fuel

The Bill Holmes story

Bill was based in Kampala as the maintenance manager of Caltex Service Station Equipment. He and his wife Peggy had a guest room where they kindly accommodated me at weekends. I was a travelling salesman for the company at that time.

In 1963, Bill was made redundant around the time that Kenya, Uganda and Tanzania gained political independence. He sub-contracted tank installations for Caltex for some months then displayed a genius for seeing and exploiting an opportunity. He was in the Mombasa club lounge in November 1965 when he spotted in a newspaper being read by someone else, that S. Rhodesia had declared Unilateral Independence from the UK.

Bill had also just learned that Caltex had put their Mombasa drum cleaning factory up for sale having switched to bulk tanker deliveries. He realised that the newly independent black, Northern Rhodesian copper mines fuel supply route via white S. Rhodesia could be politically compromised. Could their President Kaunda rely on the new, white, S. Rhodesian government to continue supplies?

Back in Mombasa, Bill, knew that a huge fleet of seven-ton trucks had just completed a local contract, researched a hire price with the owners, fuel prices with Caltex and a knock-down price for the drum cleaning factory. Then, Bill proposed a seemingly preposterous plan to his friendly Mombasa bank manager. If Bill could negotiate a profitable contract with President Kaunda to supply his mines in drums via the Great North Road, would the bank fund Bill's purchase of the factory? And would the bank fly Bill down to Lusaka to meet Kaunda?

President Kaunda signed a contract for three years with the company Bill had set up with the Bank. Bill then purchased the drum cleaning factory, hired the trucks, and began deliveries, each truck loaded with fuel filled drums.

On completion of the contract, Bill was able to purchase a fine, old, colonial house on the Mombasa sea front just as President Kenyata was 'collecting' choice properties in Kenya for his personal use. Bill thought his house was next when Kenyata's office phoned to ask if the President might visit him for tea. It turned out that Kenyata had worked there as a child and had heard that Bill was an exemplary employer at his drum factory. For Kenyata, it was just a nostalgic visit.

Bill had a new Bentley limousine shipped out from the UK. Years later, I was able to return hospitality to Bill who gave a tourmaline ring to Rosemary as a memento of our long friendship.

Brother John and I, Caltex Uganda around 1961

Peter Attwood after miraculously recovering from a car accident that left him in a coma for a year, he remarried and lectured at a Dutch university

As a young bachelor, it was very supportive to have close, reliable friends. Cedric and Anne Gunson were such in Uganda – Sadly, Anne is no longer with us.

Mike and Jean Andrews and family, friends in Kenya, have always been hugely hospitable.

At times, I don't know what I would have done without them all.

1960: Kenya and The Peter Attwood story

My second leave involved research on behalf of my great Caltex Oil friend Peter Attwood. Peter was our Lubricant Engineer advising us salesmen in relation to customers' technical applications. We played hockey together in our Nairobi Caltex team. He had his neck broken in a car accident and was shipped to the UK in a coma. During many months as I filled various assignments around East Africa, I wrote Peter infrequent but regular air-letters. Now here's the key to the unfolding drama. Peter's elderly mother, living by the Thames, continually prayed for his recovery despite the awful prognosis as to his survival.

After some time, I received an air-mail from Peter in spidery writing with the news that he had – as he put it, "woken up, still partially paralysed with my academic memory intact but with memories of earlier days of my life very vague." All this had been too much for his wife, who left him. She had received Peter's death insurance so bad had been his prognosis! I visited Peter at his mother's home from where he was bravely working as a petrol station pump assistant. He had managed to buy a new little Skoda car and asked if I would visit friends from his Edinburgh University days to learn what they used to get up to.

On this trip north, my parents joined me to visit my mother's relatives (as in days past) while I listened and noted all that Peter's chums told me. In Caltex, we never realised Peter had been the youngest ever engineering professor at the University, leaving for Kenya to give his two young sons some sunshine. I drove him for various interviews, one of which led to a lecturing appointment in India. There, he struck up a pen-pal relationship with a lovely UK Overseas Services lady and they married. Eventually, Peter became University lecturer of Engineering at Leiden University in Holland. My job was done.

Between home leaves I enormously enjoyed seven years working in various marketing positions for Caltex Oil Co across East Africa. Work life was unpressurised and related to sales through service stations and to consumer customers. This all involved a lot of business and personal driving and numerous friendships with customers of various nationalities.

Victor Sylvester dance music in a thunderstorm

Here I digress to confess my fondness for cars. There were company cars – reliable Peugeots (203 and 403), VW Beetles, an Opel, a Morris Traveller and a Mercedes 190. Then, at the same time there were personal favourites, purchased for a song from departing Government officials at the end of their three year tour of duty: a Jaguar Mark 7 limousine, an Alvis P14 and – the love of my life – a tired, cream 1952 MG TD sports two seater purchased for £100 from a friend, Mike Farey. This MG had a dysfunctional American Autovox car radio for which I paid Mike £5 in the hope of getting it to work. I was to pay him an additional £5 if I ever got it operating properly. It was 'fixed' when I hit a huge pothole and

Victor Sylvester came on the BBC world service. This was at 2.00 am in the morning by Timbarua at 8,000 feet altitude in a thunderstorm. I was delighted to hand over the extra £5 to my pal Mike.

I have a CD of a 1950s singing group called Trio Los Paraguayos which I first heard in my company VW between Kampala and Mbale in Uganda. This was on a Supersonic radio (made in Rhodesia or South Africa) which I had purchased from the Nairobi office of my good friends the Andrews family. After the usual banter, Mike's Dad, Andy Andrews, assured me I was getting it at "special discount"!

There was great camaraderie between us marketing men in Caltex. We had great management personalities, particularly our M.D., ex-Indian Army Colonel Rupert Mayne, who was very good to me. One anecdote involved me catching the wrong paddle steamer and temporarily incurring the wrath of a colleague's wife.

The wrong paddle steamer

It is said that "The Christian who avoids mistakes is one who continually consults the Lord before taking action." It is a rule that independent spirits like me seem to take ages to learn. There was a time when I didn't seem to ask anyone's advice about anything. As an example, around 1959, I took my boss on a Nile paddle steamer, for a treat.

I had suggested it as a short cut, return journey to our base in Kampala from N.E. Uganda. The idea was good: a comfortable overnight steamer trip then just 100 miles on the road instead of the normal 250 mile route along poor roads. We loaded my car aboard and sat down to an evening meal in the quaint dining saloon as the steamer paddled its way gently down the Nile. All very pleasant until we learned that this steamer would spend the following day unloading cargo at a Congo port. If only I had checked.

For me, trusting God for guidance has been an ongoing challenge. Lessons can be learned from people of faith who have gone before us. Proverbs 3v5-8 promises that if we commit our way to God not leaning just on our own understanding but trusting Him, he will direct our paths. Few Christians have lived closer to Christ than the great helper of orphans George Müller of Bristol. Trusting totally on God for supplies, without ever appealing to the public for help, he kept thousands of orphans fed for half a century. He wrote this of his experiences:

"I never remember in all my Christian course, a period now of sixty-nine years and four months, that I ever sincerely and patiently sought to know the will of God by the teaching of the Holy Ghost, through the instrumentality of the word of God, but I have always been directed rightly. But, if honesty of heart and uprightness before God were lacking, or if I did not patiently wait before God for instruction, or if I preferred the counsel of my fellow-men to the declarations of the word of the Living God, I made great mistakes."

We are not all such giants of faith. but there are many, brief, bible based, daily reading notes available in print or on-line. They can help us to check we are 'on the right steamer' of life. (Sources: Romans 8v28, Ephesians lvll & George Müller.)

Let's return to my days with Caltex in East Africa. Our retail business mainly involved service stations generally tenanted by Indians – descendants of railway construction crews who we British had imported into Kenya to help build the Mombasa to Lake Victoria "Lunatic Express" between 1897 and 1905. Our Direct Consumer customers were such as Government departments, various contractors and European settler-farmers. Social life and friendships mainly revolved around the European Sports and Social Clubs that existed, together with a church, wherever one was based.

I will always be indebted to the friendship of families during these East African years. Among many of them remain the Gunsons, Stephens, McLeods and Mackays in Uganda; the Andrews, Mowats and Rabbiosies in Kenya and the Phelps family in Tanganyika.

Take your seats – an evening concert in the bush

Feeling safe and secure is a state of mind and heart that we probably most lack in these days of the Pandemic. There is a bible promise in Jeremiah 6v16 that suggests that old fashioned ways can help us to find peace of heart and mind. "Stand at the crossroads and look; ask for the ancient paths, ask where the good way is, and walk in it, and you will find rest for your souls." I have happy memories of friends who illustrated this truth as follows:

My tale is about the Stephens family in 1958. They had worked for the British Colonial Service in Uganda for over thirty years and welcomed me as an old school friend of their son Mike.

Their home was on an agricultural seed research station. Like many British overseas, they had used local materials to build a spacious house. Over the years they had brought up a family of four and made the home comfortable. The father, Arthur Stephens owned a fine collection of original, heavy gramophone records. He had subscribed for years to a club that regularly sent him records in a wooden crate by sea mail.

His pride and joy was an HMV wind up gramophone with a huge sound horn. It used wooden needles and a special clipper ensured a fine point for each record played. The softness of these needles had protected his records. They were in good condition and the quality of sound provided me with a peaceful end to a long day of travel.

Arthur's collection extended to a large number of recordings of orchestras and soloists who I had known by repute but never heard. These old records were too heavy for him to ship back to the UK on his retirement. He was, however, able to capture the whole collection on tape when the family gave him a new reel-to-reel tape recorder.

These precious experiences were most pleasant, but for the growing realisation that African nations were soon bound to achieve Political Independence and one had better make plans for the future.

In the meantime, while in Uganda, I had been able to donate and install redundant 500 gallon petrol tanks for two Christian mission stations and an unusual inn. The Williams family at one of the missions awakened my personal Christian faith. Another was donated to a Roman Catholic Mission Hospital at Kalongo in the extreme north of Uganda.

A guiding light in the bush at night

I once made an evening journey which had a profound impact on my life. It was at a time when I had made a foolish, immoral decision that put me into an emotional wilderness for some years.

A letter had arrived at the oil company depot for which I was responsible. It was from a Catholic mission hospital on the Uganda/Sudan border enquiring whether my company would visit them to discuss supplying their fuel needs by bulk tank truck. I had permission from my company to give them a surplus underground tank and I needed to visit and inspect the location for the installation.

I thought I was allowing sufficient time to visit and return before dark. The route was new to me and the road became a track which made slow going. Suddenly it was dark, I was in the bush and there was still no sign of this mission.

Then I saw a light ahead and I was mystified that it was taking me so long to reach it. Soon, I realised that the light was much higher than the plain across which I was motoring. Indeed, it suddenly turned out to be an illuminated cross on top of a lone, low hill and below it stood the mission hospital. On later reflection, this cross and the warm welcome I received was a metaphor for the solution to my wayward ways. Regrettably, it would take some years for me to realise the significance of Christ's cross and God's offer of loving forgiveness and new life.

A week previous, I had cabled my intention to visit them and I was warmly welcomed by the Father/Doctor in charge. He gave me a warm hand-shake of welcome, drew me into their communal lounge and immediately offered me a glass of wine. This particular order of their church apparently only allow the staff to enjoy wine with visitors of which they had very few! They kindly accommodated me overnight and we were able to assist with fuel deliveries.

Their illuminated cross had transformed my journey just as faith in Christ's cross would later transform my life. Peace and joy was to follow through the reading of God's word, prayer and fellowship with other Christians – life on a totally different plain.

Another tank was gifted to an extraordinary Italian lady Toni Nuti. Her river island inn was in Western Uganda. She was a friend of Game Ranger Douglas Jones. As I shall tell, he joined me years later when the two of us temporarily worked at the Department of Trade and Industry, in Westminster London, during the 1973 Oil Crisis.

Hostess Tony Nuti, Game Warden Douglas Jones & the Shell Co 'Good Samaritan'

These friends had contrasting backgrounds – Toni came from Italy between World Wars one and two. She and her lover had eloped from disapproving parents to seek their fortunes in East Africa. They mined silver at Kikagati on the Kagera River which flows through western Uganda, from the Ruwenzori Mountains to Lake Victoria until her husband died of malaria. Undaunted, Toni became Employment Agent for the western Ugandan King of Ankoli. She arranged secure employment for his people on a huge Indian owned sugar estate between Jinja and Kampala. The King rewarded her with retirement on his secluded island where she built a beautiful bungalow and furnished it with antique furniture and paintings from her reconciled Italian family.

Douglas Jones from Surrey entered the Uganda Police in the 1940s, then transferred to the Game Department and latterly to guard white rhino in a game park adjacent to Toni's island. The island was reached by driving off the main road along bush tracks to Toni's river bank car park. There you announced your arrival by clanging a bell. You were then pulled over the torrent in a tiny open cable car once Toni had identified you. A cable seat was the only means of crossing the rushing Kagera waters until Douglas Jones built her a bridge. Douglas would bring her all sorts of orphaned, baby animals to recover before release back into the wild. In the meantime, Toni's island home became a secret B&B for selected friends including myself who arranged, for her, the installation of a surplus Caltex Oil Co underground petrol tank.

It was an extraordinary place to spend the night because it became a naturalists' paradise. Approaching the island through the bush near the town of Mbarara, the track sloped down and first sight of the island reminded one of the early Tarzan films with great trees from which vines hung and all manner of flora and fauna were at home. Toni insisted that guests dress for dinner where the company could include visitors from around the world, the table laid with Zanzibar silver. A huge Ridgeback dog dozed by a fire lit in the open grate, accompanied by a tiny orphaned Klipspringer gazelle.

The writer, H. Ryder Haggard is reputed to have based his novel "King Solomon's Mines" on this area of Uganda with its magnificent Usambara Mountains in the north-west corner of Uganda, sometimes topped with ice that glints in moonlight leading to them being called "Mountains of the Moon". One had to be personally known and liked by Toni for her to provide an evening meal and bed. Once accommodated, it was a never-to-be-forgotten experience in comfort with the sound of the river rushing by on each side of the island.

Heaven

"Watch out for Nelson and Hornblower if you stroll on the lawn before you go to bed!" warned my hostess. "Who?" we asked. "Two hippos who come up out of the river at night" she explained.

With this advice, Toni Nuti would bid me and her other guests goodnight after we had enjoyed an evening which was out of this world.

Each of us had heard of Toni's island in western Uganda by word of mouth. Some had come from Europe to see its rare birds and monkeys. Friends in Kampala had suggested I stay there on my long journeys to a client further west. None of us had expected its total difference to anything we had previously experienced.

We dined to stimulating conversation in surroundings of original paintings and carpets from Arabia. An orphaned baby antelope wandered around the table. We retired for the night to comfortable beds with beautiful linen and curtains and the gentle roar of the river. I shone a torch out of my window and, sure enough, there they were, Nelson and Hornblower. Beyond was miles of African bush. What a contrast.

Whenever I read of heaven in the Bible, Toni's island helps me to understand that it will be sublimely different to anything we have ever experienced. It says “No eye has seen, no ear has heard, no mind has conceived what God has prepared for those who love him.” (Scripture reference: 1 Corinthians 2v9)

1961: Moroto, eastern Uganda – A classic British Empire outpost and – a real drama

Some ‘Overseas Funding’ organisation had financed a huge dam construction project here. It involved heavy, earth-moving equipment. My company, Caltex, won the contract to supply large volumes of related fuel and lubricants and I serviced the account. I always enjoyed these visits as Moroto was located in a cool, highland area with most amenable, local government officials.

The Public Works Department (PWD) official supervised the Italian dam building contractors. He worked out of a little white-washed office complex shared with the local ADC – Assistant District Commissioner, the Police Superintendent and the Agricultural Officer. A flagpole and Union-Jack were located in a small quadrangle. During one of my meetings with the PWD man, he needed to communicate with a colleague across the quad. He called for a messenger who was seated in the shade outside who came in with a small cleft stick into which the PWD man placed a written note. The messenger trotted off to an office across the quad and soon returned with the written reply in the same cleft stick then returned to his seat on the verandah.

I've often thought back on how one should have learned a lesson from how men such as this messenger were content just sitting still, unworried by the passing of time. They just 'lived' when we insist on bustling about, uncomfortable unless we are doing something.

Another lesson that I remember from local Africans, was at Nairobi station. After I had left my carriage, a train attendant chased after me with my wallet which had fallen out of my pocket under a seat where he had begun to sweep. It contained more cash than he would have earned in a year. What honesty and humility, which I was glad to recognise appropriately.

The Moroto officials and their wives pretty-well comprised the local white population. I occasionally provided a film night for them in their tiny club, putting on a full-length film with a 16mm projector. On one such evening, I thought I was besieged by mosquitoes when in fact, I had fallen asleep, the drive belt to the take-up film spool had broken and filmstrip was piling up on the floor and against my leg.

The local Karamajong tribe wore absolutely no clothes but took great pride in elaborate hair-dos held together by dung. Perched on one shoulder was a small, wooden stool which also served as a pillow to safeguard their hair-do at night. They were never without a spear and shield which helped them protect their herds against neighbouring tribes except when 'shifta' rustlers entered the area with firearms. On one such occasion, a friend of mine had a truly dramatic encounter with these thugs.

Alan Howitt spotted them when he was being piloted in a small aircraft and flew down to better observe them. One of them fired 'a shot at a venture' and the bullet went up through the door of the plane, smashed Alan's jaw and embedded itself in the back of his skull. In his own words, Alan recalls how his injuries were immediately attended to locally; how he received blood at Moroto; then miraculously, surgery by visiting physicians at Mulago hospital, Kampala. Alan, finally, tells how his wife Nancy took over his contacting work in the mean time.

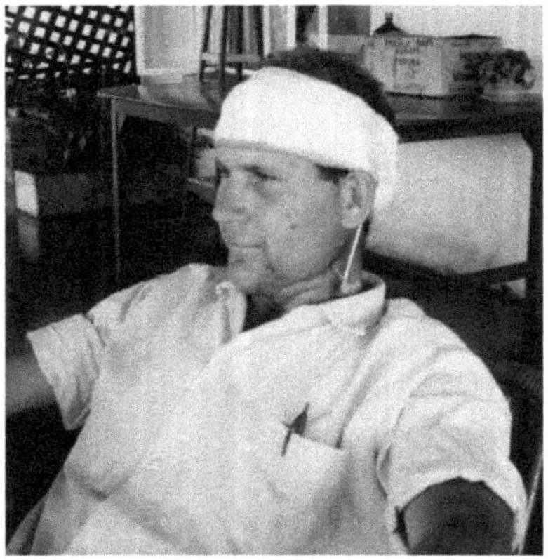
Alan recovering

Nancy shopping

“We were building a Lodge, here at the time, and my friend Ian remembered the very first Tourist had just booked in and signed the register as Doctor something and it happened to be a young woman who had just graduated and wanted to get away from everything and have a break. She had nothing medical with her. Realising that I was unable to breath she called for a razor blade. I reached into my pocket and pulled out my razor-sharp pen knife (that Nancy gave me before we were married as she knew that I liked knives). She gave me a tracheotomy and then with some cotton and needle, no anaesthetic, she stemmed the bleeding. Back into the plane with Doctor and Nancy and we had to land in Moroto as it was getting dark and this plane was not to fly at night. I had lost a critical amount of blood by this time so at the Moroto dispensary with a Peace Corps girl, they went to the neighbouring prison where they bled a few prisoners and put the drip into me. They lit the gravel runway up with vehicle lights so that the Police plane could land. We arrived at Mulago Hospital at midnight. My ninth rib replaced my jaw. I was fed through a tube, and had Plaster of Paris around my head to keep it together. My employer Frank was away in Australia so Nancy had to run the whole show, including paying all the staff. We had truck drivers, tractor drivers and many builders – a very big staff. As Nancy was working in the Tororo Bank at the time she was able to draw the wages. Then she had to travel to all the building and road sites in Karamoja and Gulu."

This 2020 Christmas, I e-mailed my good wishes to Alan in Australia.

My memories now move from Uganda to the Island of Zanzibar off the coast of Tanzania. It was the scene of particular savagery in the early 1960s before becoming part of the newly Independent Tanzania.

1964: The Massacre on Slavery Island

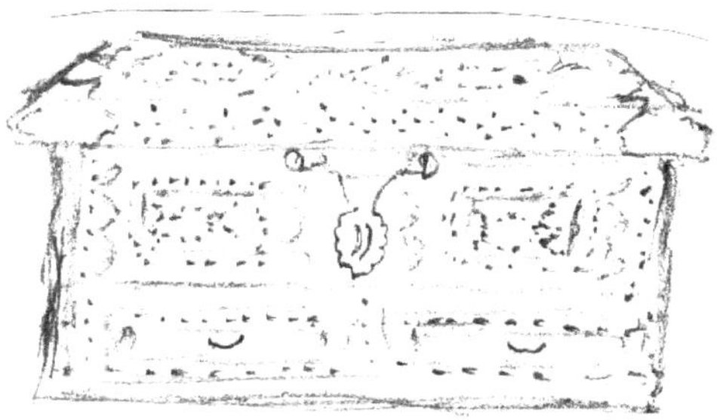

Zanzibar has a turbulent history of involvement in the slave trade. I have a memento of that island in the form of an Arab chest.

Zanzibar is an island in the Indian Ocean just 10 miles off the coast of East Africa. The British were primarily responsible for closing the Arab slave market which had operated there for most of the nineteenth century. A few fortunate Africans had met men like Livingstone who literally freed them from chains.

During political upheaval in the 1960s, African residents on Zanzibar slaughtered its Arab population. Just after this massacre, I visited my employer's oil company tank depot on Zanzibar. The tourist market which had replaced the slave market was also closed and the governing regime was oppressive.

Despite all this, a brave young African businessman discreetly caught my attention and showed me a humble chest he had made. I had always wanted a brass decorated Arab chest. Now that they were no more, I agreed to buy this next-best-thing, if he could get it to my cabin on the Union Castle ship out in the harbour. Somehow he succeeded and the chest now stands in our Lyme Regis home. That chest has me thinking of personally being set free from past sin and foolishness through faith in Christ. I can look at that chest and know that as a Christian, Christ is with me and has set me free from being "held in slavery by the fear of death." (Sources: Romans 3v24 and Hebrews 2v14-15.)

5. 1966-1973: University; Chevron Oil (UK) Ltd; the DTI, Westminster

1966: Strathclyde University, Glasgow

1966, Oh my! Glasgow is cold and MBA studies at Strathclyde University a challenge.

In 1966, I reluctantly left East Africa for a one-year introductory MBA course at Strathclyde University, Glasgow to 'bridge me over' from colonial to UK employment. This entailed the shocking down to earth transition from marketing in the sunshine to student accommodation and studies in cold Scotland. I had however arrived six months too early for the course. Fortune favoured me with an Advertising and Sales Promotion assignment with BP Scotland. Their Advertising and Sales Promotion Manager had had a heart attack just before a major campaign launch and they asked me to help them out.

At this time, I was asked to referee a football match on a muddy pitch and I aggravated an old knee injury which required surgery. I was blessed with great kindness by the Porteous family at their lovely Helensburgh home by the Clyde, which helped my recovery. Their son Bob had joined BP after a period with the Scots Guards. He, myself and another BP colleague, Irishman Ned Stokes, later chummed up for some good times together.

The management of BP were sufficiently impressed with my work that they invited me to return to them after my year at Strathclyde. When I expressed an interest in returning overseas, they kindly arranged an interview for me with Shell International which I attended but I was fated never to join them. The person interviewing me had been a marketing rep for Shell in the same Kenya area where I had represented Caltex. I had taken a large customer from him! Instead of giving me the benefit of fair hearing, he took exception and my interview was unsuccessful. Only a week later, I was on the London tube when I met another Shell competitor from my Caltex days in Uganda who had also become a friend. He said he had replaced my interviewer just days after my interview and that the outcome could have been quite different. Actually, and on reflection, this 'colonial type' would never have fitted into the exclusive, Oxbridge 'Shell Club' ethos.

Returning to my memories of Strathclyde and Glasgow, my mother was born in nearby Blantyre. Due to regular visits to see her family over the years, I was familiar with the area in general but not prepared for the changes that had begun to take place with Glasgow city itself. Nearby Greenock on the river Clyde had been a centre of shipbuilding for years, but the advent of modern passenger aircraft had brought an abrupt end to that industry. The Glasgow city authorities were, however, determined to regenerate their city and began by making it an early IT centre with the arrival of IBM from America. A few years later, the city was unrecognisable with motorways through and around it.

On the MBA (Dip) course there were students from various countries who already had degrees and I chummed up with Yayier Maiver from Israel and George Carmanos from Australia. We had one memorable session with IBM who had just arrived in the UK. They set us a hypothetical business challenge. It was before the days of personal computers. They fed our solution into – wait for it – an IBM MAINFRAME computer, that spewed out data showing the errors in our propositions!

Chevron Oil (UK) Ltd.

That year's course at Strathclyde University flew by. On the back of it and my previous Caltex Oil Co experience I was fortunate to join and enjoy working, for seven years, with Chevron Oil (U.K.) Ltd, a company distantly related to Caltex. Chevron purchased Service Stations from the UK, Regent Oil Co. Responsible for

Advertising and Sales Promotion, I enjoyed pleasant colleagues and working with them, I spent six years helping to establish this ‘brand’ before our assets were taken over and re-branded Texaco. My boss and close friend was John Parkman. He and wife Sonia often made me welcome at their lovely country home in Kent.

Our recently arrived American Chevron owners were set on introducing traditional State-side, ‘five point’ forecourt service at the service stations they had purchased from Regent Oil. While one attendant supplied petrol, another was to clean the windscreen and offer to check tyre pressures, radiator water and engine oil levels – all in the hope of associated sales. Well, we soon fell at the first hurdle. Customers left feedback such as “No thanks. I had my windscreen rubbed with an oily cloth in 1941 and it took me ages to clean off”!

During this time, an extraordinary ‘Game Changer’, entrepreneur named Gerald Ronson entered the domestic retail scene to revolutionise it in the UK and America. Having inherited substantial wealth, he spotted an opportunity in the UK, related to Green Shield Stamp franchises held by independent, petrol filling stations in London around the North and South Circular roads. These stations were attracting commercial travellers by offering ‘four-fold’ stamps against which those customers’ wives could redeem household gifts.

Mr Ronson purchased a large number of these little stations, covered the pumps with a large illuminated canopy and built stylish and well stocked accessory sales kiosks, plus loos. Then – WAIT FOR IT – he made customers serve themselves at the pumps! Appreciating the four-fold stamps and the shopping convenience of the kiosks, custom poured in to these new stations that sparkled clean around the clock. As their volume of petrol sales boomed, Mr Ronson was reputed to arrive to inspect these stations repeatedly. He rewarded staff with a £10 note if the station met his standards or, alternatively, a notice of dismissal if they did not. He then sold the whole group of these stations to Shell Oil for an undisclosed amount.

The American oil companies were watching this forecourt revolution and it was not long before Self Service began to appear at many of their service stations.

Among our non-American Chevron colleagues, I fondly remember New-Zealander, John Henley and especially his surprising 21st birthday present to his son. The young man woke to find a birthday card by his bed with a string attached. The string meandered all over the house from the loft to the basement ending up attached to the ignition key in an MG Midget sports car in the garage. What delight – and a metaphor of how we can be inclined to underestimate our Father God's love for us as individuals.

1973: Department of Trade and Industry oil industry adviser during the OPEC oil crisis

This assignment was an interesting challenge made special by three extraordinary coincidences that happened while I was there.

The DTI needed temporary clerical help during the crisis. One of the recruits was Douglas Jones, the sixty year old colonial legend about whom I have already written. Recently thrown out of Uganda by the monstrous Idi Amin, he had been managing the preservation of white rhinos near the Kagera River island of Toni

Nuti in western Uganda when he was deported. Who should I bump into at the same DTI building but Douglas Jones. Douglas had sadly driven a very ill Toni to a Nairobi hospital where she died. He was prevented from re-entering Uganda by Idi Amin's guards, so here he was, keeping the wolf from the door, working at the DTI as a temporary clerk. Aged well into his seventies, it was his first visit to the UK in twenty years. The suits he had left with his sister twenty years before still fitted him.

My weeks at the DTI brought me three special blessings:

Firstly, Douglas and I joyously reminisced during our lunch hours together.

Secondly, these weeks at the DTI exactly coincided with my dear old father's final days of treatment at the Royal Marsden Hospital, London. I was able to spare him ambulance transport and drive him to and from his Sydenham home which was on my own daily route.

Thirdly, by helping a particular Shell executive to sort out problems caused by certain heating oil distributors who had attempted to evade VAT, I was able to repay this man's kindness to me in Kenya seventeen years previously. I immediately recognised his double-barrel name and very proper accent. During my 1956 school rugby tour of the Kenya Highland, my farmer host at Eldoret was to drive me to Kitale. He neglected to tie down my little suitcase on his roof rack and it was absent on our arrival, late at night, at Kitale. My host there was this same Shell man. He immediately drove me back along the rough, dirt road in his new, long-wheelbase Land Rover. There, sticking up out of a ditch was my suitcase. Here, over the DTI phone, I had re-connected with my Shell Good Samaritan. Small world!

Before the sale of Chevron to Texaco, I was privileged to have this DTI assignment. It involved investigating claims by some domestic oil heating distributors that their DTI crisis rations were set unfairly low against their normal off-take from their respective supplying oil companies. I discovered that some distributors proved (to their subsequent embarrassment) that their total deliveries to care homes etc., were greater than the volumes they had previously drawn under their oil co contracts. Investigations found that they had been illegally dodging UK tax by purchasing from small, smuggler tankers moving between Rotterdam and Thames ports. But how was I to discover this?

My bulldog clip angel

At the DTI, I had been allocated an empty, ex-cloakroom, with a table, chair, a telephone and an empty three-drawer filing cabinet. No P.C.s at that time. To my rescue came a wise, elderly civil servant who helped me with a map of the districts of the Greater London area which he set up on an old blackboard. He numbered the coat hooks around the walls, each number representing a district. He went out and procured a large bulldog clip for each hanger. We gave each incoming claim its appropriate district number and hung each claim on its clip.

A pattern emerged as the clips of the districts nearest the Thames began to fill up. We phoned the sales managers of the oil companies supplying these distributors. They in turn cross-questioned the distributors as to where they might be obtaining their excess gallonage and the illicit, tax-dodging truth emerged. The senior DTI manager to whom I was reporting subsequently wrote a kind letter of commendation to my own employers saying what a fine job I had done for the DTI!

6. 1974-81: Conversion to Christianity; Bible College; Radio Broadcasting Seychelles

The period 1971 through 1973 involved such radical changes in my life that I remember it as a bit of a blur. The Revd. Stanley Voke, was pastor of the Baptist Church adjacent to my home in Walton-on-Thames Surrey. He had regularly delivered the "Challenge" Christian newspaper to me. Because of our common background – Africa and my missionary parents, he would encourage me to seriously consider the necessity of realising I needed forgiveness for my sins through believing in Jesus Christ.

The London accountant and the African bush bee keeper

I shared my Walton-on-Thames house with another ex-colonial, Dicker Bennent. He told an amusing true story against himself. On qualifying as an accountant, he visited his widowed mother at Dar-es-Salaam on the Tanzanian coast. He had not seen her during his five years qualifying. Having just completed his articles, he could only afford the flight to Nairobi in Kenya. He then planned to hitchhike to Dar-es-Salaam.

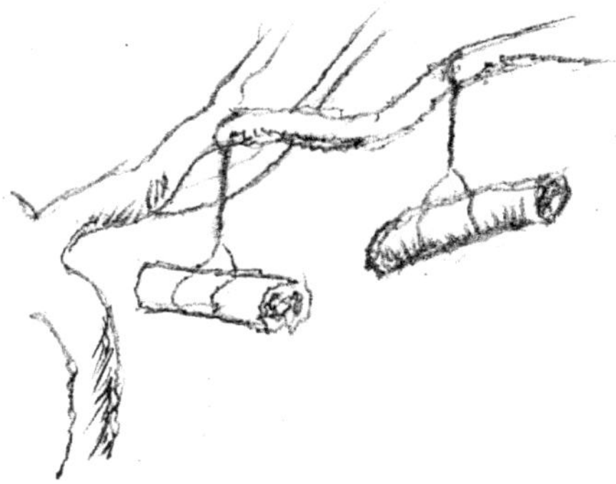

Dicker overlooked the facts that both countries had achieved political independence during his absence. No longer were there white commercial travellers and he found himself stranded in the bush after a short lift on an African truck. He started to walk when a voice called "Jambo" – hello – from under a tree loaded with African bee hives high in its branches.

Beginning to feel embarrassed, Dicker returned the greeting knowing that the African would next ask his destination. Walking on, Dicker answered "Dar-es-Salaam". The African was astonished at seeing this young mzungu (white), hatless with a small suitcase, hoping for a lift. The beekeeper waited some moments then volunteered the single Kiswahili word "pole" (pronounced 'polé'). Now this is one of the classic Kiswahili words with multiple uses. It can be used to caution or to recommend care or in sympathy towards a fallen child or, as in this case, towards someone who is clearly in difficulty or perhaps having a mental aberration.

By now, Dicker was too far away to continue the conversation and most fortunate that someone soon gave him a lift right to his destination. He never told me how he returned to the UK.

It just so happened that during August 1971, I visited New Jersey, USA for the wedding of my nephew Barry Durman to his fiancée Joanne. One Sunday, during that visit, I heard the clear Bible teaching of their pastor Charles Anderson. He confirmed in no uncertain terms my need to personally make my peace with God through faith in His Son the Lord Jesus Christ. I there and then invited Christ into my heart to be my Saviour and Lord. This resulted from an instantaneous and powerful conviction and regret about certain aspects of my past life. I returned much chastened to my work with Chevron Oil just prior to the aforementioned secondment into the DTI when I was struck by two realisations:

1. The 1971 OPEC driven Oil crisis would permanently change my kind of domestic marketing;
2. I needed somehow to obtain serious instruction in Bible knowledge and church history.

Dear Stanley Voke got a real surprise to see me in his congregation on my return. He and new church friends like Peter and Mac Thompsett began to deepen my involvement in the fellowship, my personal commitment to Christ and the work of God's Holy Spirit in my life. I felt a call to a period of full time study and extraordinary incidents (again) firmly led me to the Bible College of Wales for its 1974 session. A friend had read "Rees Howells Intercessor" about its founder and I was about to enter the most pivotal year of my life.

Seven happy years with Chevron Oil Co (UK) Ltd before…

...1974 at the wonderful Bible College of Wales under Principal Revd. Samuel Howells majoring on faith in Christ and prayer.

Revd. Stanley and Mrs Doreen Voke. He was an exceptional bible teacher.

Here I am with Nazmi from Iraq (left). (right) Toshio and Massa from Japan & Benni from Ghana. These four were my inspirational fellow students and pals at the Bible College of Wales, Swansea.

Nazmi had escaped with his life from an Islamic home after a vision of Christ. The other three and I formed a harmony singing group which apparently sounded pretty good.

Winding back for a moment to Walton, here is ex RAF pilot Clifford Luxton. We had a special Sunday School going for gypsy children.

See the account (to follow) of how a dying young German pilot remarkably strengthened Clifford's faith during his exhausting night flights carrying resistance fighters in and out of France.

Rosemary with Peter and Mac Thompsett who 'discipled' me during the early days of my Christian pilgrimage (when Peter and I were also searching for MG spare parts). We remain great friends to this day.

Bible college

The history of Christianity records people of extraordinary faith in God experiencing great answers to their prayers. Examples were Elijah and Daniel in the Old Testament and the Apostles and Jesus himself in the New Testament. In the twentieth century, George Müller fed thousands of Bristol orphans, and Rees Howells, then his son Samuel, financed the Bible College of Wales for eighty years without ever appealing for help except through Bible inspired, persistent and believing prayer in the name of the Lord Jesus Christ. Whenever they encountered any resistance to the spread of the Gospel of Christ, they spoke of and practised “gaining a position of spiritual authority through persevering prayer to pull down that interference” no matter how great that obstacle might be.

On arrival at the Bible college of Wales, I soon made sound friendships with other students Toshio and Massa from Japan, Benny from Ghana and Nazmi from Turkey. Each of these arrived having even more unusual pilgrimages than my own. We formed a group to help lead college worship with yours truly on guitar and four of us singing in harmony. We apparently sounded pretty good. Lecturers were inspiring but it was the evening prayer meetings that I will never forget. Led by Principal ‘Mr Samuel’ and eminent visitors, prayers were inspired by scriptures relevant to college, parochial or global matters that were on the hearts of the college at the time. They were ‘prayed through’ sometimes over extended periods of such meetings, until God answered in one way or another. That year gave me undoubted faith in that type of praying as taught by Christ himself in Luke chapter 11v1-13. So close to God were the staff during the second world war and so clearly did the Holy Spirit direct their prayers that diaries record clear connections between the positive outcome of certain battles and their prayers for our forces BEFORE such incidents were made public. A particular example relates to the college praying for protection for Jews in Palestine against an alliance between Arabs and Germany to crush those Jews. At the Battle of El

Alamein, advancing, dry-mouthed, parched German troops overran a British storage depot whilst trying to get to Alexandria. They shot holes in water pipes that had just been laid and gulped away, not realising that the pipes contained salty sea water used to test the system before it was put into use. They became so ill that they surrendered, their advance halted. Prayers answered.

When I joined the college in 1974/5, there were no fees as such but we worked in various departments to earn our way. I found myself up at 5.00am, lighting the coke oven in the bakery and learning from William Rowlands the baker, to provide loaves and other items for the college staff and students.

On Sundays, we were sent out to preach at various churches and I remain grateful for many friendships made during such visits especially with the Paloha family in Aberdare.

The spiritual ethos of the Bible College of Wales

The essential quality of the Bible College of Wales was, to me, **the Spiritual Chemistry of the place**. I felt that I was was a phony student. I had money in the bank. I was never tested 'to pray for a postage stamp' or all other needs as with some other students who really were living by faith for all their needs. In retrospect, I would liken myself to the disciple Peter who, though he had met Jesus, only later came to fully realise Christ's salvation. In my case, God used the examples of the staff and students to leave indelible, spiritual examples to me of where I was falling short in terms of holiness and real love. I still reflect back on them all with the greatest gratitude and most humbling preparation for what service God has had me stumble through ever since.

The other 'sharpening' tool the Lord used on me was gaining a deeper experience of personal prayer, often out of bed in the night with an eiderdown around me in the unheated building. This ex-oil executive was 'going through the mill'. **Benni from Ghana** was just one example. When I once asked him what he hoped for after college, I expected him to be aspiring to a be a teacher or preacher. Instead, clasping his hands together, he said "I want to always be so close to Jesus that **nothing** will come between him and me". Each student or staff member imprinted something memorable onto my spiritual DNA which I did not realise at the time. **that** was all part of the **unique Spiritual Chemistry of the place** from Mr Samuel himself to the most humble student. **It** was the crucial, pivotal point in my whole life. **Priceless**.

A remarkable room-mate

College principal Mr Samuel, visited me one evening and asked me to take care of, and share my double room with, a refugee who had just arrived from Turkey with little English. It turned out that Nazmi was actually Kurdish and lived by the Turkish border in Iraq with his Roman Catholic mother and Moslem father. He gradually told me that two incidents in his teens suggested that he was under some kind of peculiar protection.

The first incident occurred when he and a chum wandered with their goats into Turkey and were accosted by three armed men who had them dig their own graves. Suddenly, two of the men turned their guns on their leader and allowed them to escape. A little while later, a fortune teller was entertaining Nazmi's family but complained that he could not perform for Nazmi himself.

It appears that Nazmi's parents nominal approach to their different religions left him confused but untroubled until he met an American Christian in a cafe who gave him a Turkish Bible in which he underlined John 6v45 "I tell you the truth, he who believes has everlasting life." Nazmi received a reprimand from his father when he showed this to his parents. He went into his bedroom, threw the Bible at the wall and it fell open on his bed at this passage. In his frustration, Nazmi fell on his knees and prayed that he would wait until God showed him the truth.

Allow me to repeat what Nazmi told me happened next: "I found myself in a deep valley, threatened by a lion who I instinctively knew was Satan. I fended him off with a stout wooden staff. As I backed away up some stairs behind me to a level place, the lion followed but suddenly cowered and I turned to see Jesus Christ with a multitude of people in front of a glorious city. Jesus beckoned me in our gentle eastern way with fingers down and bid me sit before him. He told me he was sending me back to serve him on Earth then I woke up in my room.

"I was so excited and shared my dream with my parents. My father was furious and threw me out of our home. My mother found me and said I could return but must never mention Jesus again. I found the American and we reasoned that I would be in danger of my life if my father put my story about. The American had arranged and financed my escape, first to help in a Christian bookshop in Istanbul that had connections with the Bible College of Wales, then he moved me on to the college itself."

Nazmi sat by me at lectures during which I printed for him, the simplest possible summary of what was being said. The Holy Spirit gave him a remarkably rapid understanding of both lectures and English. During our quiet times, he would meditate on just a verse or two of scripture then share profound insights to encourage both of us in our Saviour and Lord Jesus Christ. He had clearly searched the scriptures before ever coming to the college and was an inspiration to me.

Nazmi had a clear premonition that he would eventually return to his homeland and give his life for the Lord. He did return to Istanbul and we kept in touch for a while. He married then, sadly, we lost touch.

A unique continuity of leadership

The Bible College of Wales has a unique continuity of leadership based on extraordinary Christian faith and prayer for all its needs. It was founded by Rees Howells in 1924.

Rees received God's command that through faith and prayer, he was to look solely to God for all college needs as well as for supporting other Christians as led by the Holy Spirit. There were to be no other appeals for financial support.

He remained Director until his death in 1950. His son, the Revd. Samuel Rees Howells, took over leadership until he handed over the college to Alan Scotland in 2002 shortly before Samuel's own death in 2004.

Mr Richard Maton served under Samuel for forty seven years, latterly as Principal of the college. Richard's wife Kristine first joined the college in 1936. Together, Richard and Kristine spent more than 120 years at the college. A number of other staff members served more than sixty years at the Bible College of Wales. It is no exaggeration to say that I was standing on sacred ground during my own period of study there.

After 2004, God has ensured further continuity of this faith and prayer based ministry but that is another story.

The coal miners

One Sunday, I was invited to preach at the Cwamdare church at Aberdare. Enroute, I got a clear indication from the Holy Spirit that I was to change my prepared text to Hebrews 2v14-15, on which I had recently meditated “Since the children have flesh and blood, he too shared in their humanity so that by his death he might destroy him who holds the power of death – that is the devil – and free those who all their lives were held in slavery by the fear of death.”

Well, the Cwamdare fellowship was lead by a Spirit filled pastor and I always felt privileged by his willingness to let me preach in his place. Now here was I, ill prepared to speak on this ‘imposed’ text but I was uplifted by the usual, encouraging prayer time in the vestry before hand. No sooner had I introduced the text when the main door opposite me opened and a group of sturdy men marched in. I had no idea that they had just come from the funeral of a fellow miner and that apparently, they were not regular church attenders.

I stumbled through my talk but afterwards, the pastor felt that I had reinforced the imposed text with the Hebrews “Man lives once to die and then the judgement” and balanced it with the additional Hebrews sufficiency of Christ's blood and forgiveness for those who believe. 'Phew'. Only the Lord knows how he will have used his word in the lives of those miners that day.

I became very close to the Paloha family of that fellowship. They had found themselves 'marooned' there when their Eastern European country closed its borders during their visit to relatives in Aberdare. God soon had them recording programmes in Eastern European languages for closed, communist countries through the Trans-World Christian Broadcasting station at Monte Carlo.

I was inspired by all of the lecturers at the college and particularly enjoyed David Davies and Ieuan Jones.

1960s: Revd David Davies, spiritual revival and rescue from rebels

The revival started like the 1904 Welsh revival. Here, during a service, a young African girl became convicted of her sin. She cried out in fear of judgement as the Holy Spirit fell on the whole congregation. During subsequent days, troubled members received encouragement from the Revd. and Mrs Davies to confess their sins and receive forgiveness through believing that Christ had been judged in their place on the cross. People of all ages found relief at this time.

A young boy had stolen a single razor blade from the counter of of a local store while he shopped for his mother. The owner was an unfriendly Greek. Nevertheless, the child returned the blade explaining the reason. The Greek patted him on the head, told him to stay honest and gave him some nuts and fruit to take home.

A lady who had supplied the Davies with eggs for years wept as she confessed that she had sometimes supplied them with eggs that she had stolen from their own chickens at the back of the house.

Revd. Davies also told of how a large mission hospital on a main road received protection from rampaging Congolese 'Simba' militia. The staff knew their compound was obvious and that robberies and worse were to be expected. They prayed around the clock for God's protection. When the dreaded convoy approached, the hospital staff saw a long row of angelic figures with hands joined, along the entire front boundary of their mission. This heavenly protection apparently hid the very existence of the mission from the rebels who drove straight past.

Revd. Davies and his wife were eventually rescued by Belgian troops. Other missionaries were murdered before they could be saved.

Revd. Davies was a very thorough Bible teacher. I still remember him deeply expounding the two chapters of the minor prophet, Haggai over a whole college term!

Revd. Ieuan Jones and God's miraculous provision of groceries

He, his wife and two small children had been expelled from China. The UK office of the China Inland Mission had apparently lacked information as to their arrival. Welsh friends provided them with an isolated cottage but they were soon without basic provisions. Despite their empty larder Revd. Jones insisted they lay the table for breakfast and began the Lord's prayer. As he got to “Give us this day our daily bread" there was a knock on the door and there was a man with a tea chest of groceries for them including an envelope containing a substantial amount of cash.

Revd. Jones turned to calm the excited children. When he turned back to express his appreciation, the man had disappeared. The Revd. walked up the drive in case a delivery vehicle was behind an adjacent hedge. This was when he noticed gravel that been laid the precious evening was undisturbed.

We were always inspired when Revd. Jones took morning prayers. He especially loved the Psalms of David.

Full-time church-related service

In 1975, I returned to assist Pastor Stanley Voke to develop youth-work at the Walton-on-Thames Baptist Church and strengthen its prayer ministry, beginning with a pre-breakfast 6.30am meeting which, remarkably, was often attended by businessmen before they travelled to their businesses in London. I was assisted by Malcolm Cordle to develop a Sunday morning Youth Service prior to the main service. Clifford Luxton encouraged me to start a separate Sunday School for gypsy children staffed by teenagers whom I trained for that purpose. Clifford lived in the same council estate where the gypsies had been housed out of their caravans. Clifford had a wonderful RAF, Christian experience. On Saturday afternoons, I took a Billy Graham "Fact and Faith" film to the Youth Prison at Feltham.

I will always remain indebted to the leadership at Walton Baptist Church namely Pastor Stanley Voke and elders Ken Griffiths, Will Lemon and Jill Reece for their encouragement and wisdom.

God speaks through a dying German airman

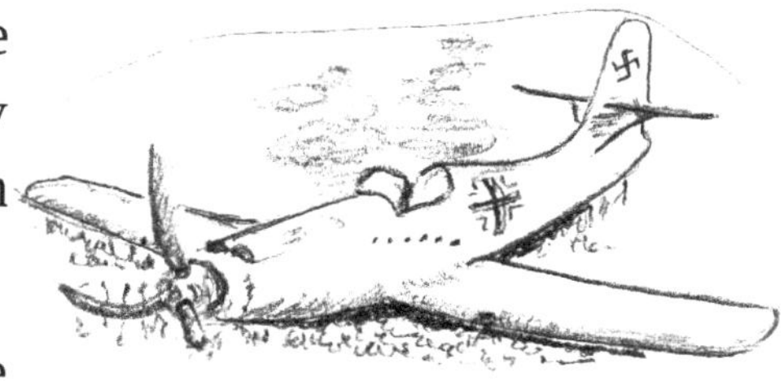

Clifford Luxton told me that as an RAF pilot, he had been flying night missions into enemy territory and was in a state of nervous exhaustion himself.

He and his Welsh co-pilot Taffy were leaving the RAF base after a briefing when a German fighter plane, the victim of a dogfight overhead, crash landed in a field at the end of their runway. Cliff gave me the following account of what then happened.

Clifford and Taffy raced to get the pilot out to safety before the smoking plane blew up.

They managed to haul the German pilot out onto the grass at a safe distance from the plane. He was obviously badly injured and apparently unconscious. They pulled off his helmet and were astonished to see that he was a blond haired, handsome young fellow of no more than 17 years of age.

As mentioned, Clifford told me that at this time he had been flying night missions into enemy territory and was in a state of nervous exhaustion himself. Although he had a firm Welsh chapel background, he had begun to feel his Christian faith weakening. He did however have a good knowledge of the Bible including the story of a boy, Samuel, in the Old Testament to whom God spoke. The lad had thought it was his priest calling him but the old man in question realised it was God. The priest told the lad, if God called again, he should answer "Speak, Lord, for your servant is listening."

When Clifford saw the youthfulness of the German pilot, he turned to Taffy and said, "He reminds me of the boy Samuel," at which the German opened his eyes and said in perfect English, "Speak, Lord, for your servant is listening," and immediately died.

From that moment, Cliff felt his faith strengthened. He flew many more missions in and out of enemy territory in small planes ferrying members of the French Resistance and British Intelligence. "I was sure," he said, "that God had mysteriously used a German Christian 'enemy' to encourage me. God had spoken to me and I never had any further doubts that He was with me for the rest of the war and that He has remained with me ever since."

(Scripture references:— l Samuel 3v1-17 and Romans 10v17)

An extraordinary hospital visit from my Walton church

All I had intended was to take comfort and some grapes to a sick church member at St Peters hospital in Chertsey. On returning to my locked van outside a Chertsey grocery, I found my Mini's driver's door handle had been forced down. I unlocked and entered via the back door only to find the starter would not function and I was running late against visiting times.

I requested help from a large man approaching along the empty pavement. He gave me a shove. The car started and I stopped to thank him but he had disappeared. I parked the car on a sloping part of the hospital car park. On reaching my friend's ward he urgently directed me to another patient who he explained was critically ill. After introducing myself as a church visitor, the old man expressed his appreciation after I prayed for him and encouraged him to trust in Jesus Christ's love for him. A bell sounded to end visiting. I waved farewell to my friend, left the building and learned later that the old man died that night.

I set my car rolling down the slope and it started. As I passed men digging a deep trench on the roadside back to Walton, a workman carelessly swung a heavy wooden beam out under my front wheel. It demolished my wheel which I replaced with my spare. I was sharing my accident with the next person on my visitation list when her neighbour overheard my tale and gave me an unwanted Mini wheel with tyre which had long languished in his garage. On reflection, I was convinced that I had been involved in an unseen drama and influenced the eternal destiny of the old man with whom I had prayed in the hospital.

Glimpses of the Healing Power of Jesus Christ

Through Baptist Church connections, I was asked to preach at other churches. Prior to one such service, I read Mark 16v20 "Then the disciples went out and preached everywhere, and the Lord worked with them and confirmed His word by the signs that accompanied it." These words inspired me to ask God to answer prayers he might give me for the sick. On no less than four subsequent occasions miraculous healing took place either for myself or others.

The first occasion involved me taking a wheelchair-bound friend with cancer to a small, independent, Christian group in Ewell, Surrey. They believed in and practised prayer for the sick according to the Bible guidance in James 5v14-15 that any sick person could "call the elders of the Church to pray over him and anoint him with oil in the name of the Lord. And the prayer offered in faith will make the sick person well. If he has sinned, he will be forgiven." In stooping to pray for my friend, the minister brushed past me and although I had not included myself for prayer, I was instantly healed of a most painful frozen shoulder. My friend received marginal relief. God works in a mysterious way!

With this still in mind, I personally offered to pray for another wheelchair-bound person at our own Walton-on-Thames Baptist Church during after-church coffee time. She had a brain tumour and had lost the use of her legs. After asking her permission, I asked God to heal her in accordance with his word in Romans 8v11 "If the Spirit of him who raised Jesus from the dead is living in you, he who raised Christ from the dead will also give life to your mortal bodies through his Spirit who lives in you." A little later, this lady found she had regained the use of her legs.

A few Sundays later, I was asked to take a service at a large Baptist fellowship in Worcester Park near Sutton, greater London. I spoke about how Jesus' disciples suggested that he send a multitude away to find something to eat and how in Mark 6v37 Christ responded "**You** give them something to eat." I suggested that we might sometimes offer more help to others than we do. I offered to pray in the name of Jesus Christ for individual needs after the service. A lady left it until Rosemary and I were in the car park before she plucked up the courage to ask for prayer about her awful depression. This we did. The following week, her husband phoned us to say "I have my wife back." Then she herself confirmed how she realised she had, for some time, harboured bitter resentment against another person. After our prayer together, she had been able to make her peace with that person and her depression lifted.

Christ then answered my prayers for four people at a small Baptist church in Farncombe near Godalming. I was about to minister the Communion sacraments when a verse came strongly to my mind from the last book in the Old Testament of the Bible – Malachi chapter 4v2 "But for you who revere my name, the sun of righteousness will rise with healing in its wings." I said I believed this looked ahead to Jesus Christ and invited members of the congregation desiring prayer for healing to come forward after the communion. I joined hands with two church deacons who had assisted with dispensing the bread and wine and we then prayed for three people who came forward. They later testified to their various needs being met. One of the two deacons who assisted me did not ask for prayer but, on returning home, he discovered himself healed of serious arthritis.

Most importantly, while helping the Pastor at this Walton fellowship, I met Church member Speech Therapist, Rosemary Barnes, who was later to become my wife.

My introduction to FEBA

One early morning prayer meeting was attended by a lady missionary on leave from the Christian, Far Eastern Broadcasting Association (FEBA) station on Mahé island of the Seychelles. She was having difficulty finding treatment for a tropical, dry eye ailment. While we prayed for her, I remembered that Dr Peter Williams, a friend from my Uganda days, had recently retired to Reading. He specialised in ophthalmics and was working as a locum at a clinic there. I called him after breakfast and he was soon able to provide drops to solve her eye problem.

While driving her to and fro, the lady missionary told me that FEBA Radio Seychelles needed someone based in Nairobi, Kenya to coordinate the production of programmes for the East Africa region. Technically, this radio station bounced shortwave signals off the stratosphere, around the globe, its ‘reach’ depending on the capability of its aerials and the power of its transmitters. I felt I had fulfilled my usefulness at Walton, I knew Kiswahili, the ‘lingua franca’ of East Africa, and since Nairobi was my original ‘home town’, I felt drawn to that opportunity. I was interviewed and accepted by FEBA on condition I could raise the necessary financial support.

This was soon forthcoming from members of the mission-minded Walton fellowship. So, off I went but, as it turned out, to be based at the Seychelles Station not Nairobi.

On first confronting these responsibilities, with my inexperience, I felt like the veritable square peg in a round hole. I had to type my own correspondence with the national studios and the scripts for my own English programmes. Remarkably and with the help of an American member of another mission on the Island, I learned to touch type in three weeks. This was all before laptops with spell check apps and doubly challenging with my dyslexia. At the end of three years I felt burned out, resigned from FEBA and returned to Walton-on-Thames. I shall always be grateful for the practical and moral support of the other missionaries on the station, particularly Norman and Janet Brierley whose home was always open house for me.

An epidemic of Dengue fever had led to the repatriation of three senior staff to the UK (hence Seychelles not Nairobi). I was to temporarily fill the Programme Controller role, liaising with staff at studios in Tanzania, Madras, Bangalore, Delhi and Bombay. They produced programmes in Kiswahili, Arabic and several Indian languages. I held that position for three years. Apart from programming, the station had both an engineering and a news department staffed by specialists from the UK. In charge of the whole operation was firstly John Wheatley who founded the station and later, engineer Dr David Bacon.

The indigenous studio staff did magnificent work often using antiquated reel-to-reel tape recorders. They provided not just evangelical Christian programmes but also health, agricultural and other general interest programmes. They invited and received encouraging feedback by letter from listeners of various religions. This reaffirmed our faith that God was using this medium to reach ‘our parish’ of unnumbered listeners despite competition from other local and international broadcasting stations.

The FEBA operation was largely funded by British and American churches since the Seychelles station was set up as an independent associate of the similar, larger American station FEBC in the Phillipines. Churches in countries such as Norway also helped to sponsor individual programmes. Politics and technological changes after my time led FEBA to depart the Seychelles shortwave operation in favour of renting time on numerous, local FM stations now broadcasting in an even greater number of languages than previously.

While I was based in the Seychelles, my job involved regular visits to the indigenous studios and listening to English translations of samples of the programmes that they were supplying for our shortwave transmitters to broadcast to their target areas. Also, I would check the strength and clarity of both the hourly English language news, and all the indigenous language programmes from the Seychelles, which we sent out to all those areas from our aerials planted on reefs off Mahé island.

A prayer for rain

There was a draught on Mahé and tanker lorries were easing water shortages. During a FEBA staff prayer meeting, our newsman Baden Hickman offered an impassioned plea on behalf of the local population. I watched clouds gather as he prayed and rain began to fall with such force on our metal roof that we had to close the meeting because of the noise.

This incident reminded me of the bible account of the prophet Elijah’s identical prayer and result as recorded in 1 Kings 18v45.

Representatives of Far Eastern Broadcasting departments, Seychelles

Here I am with Raj on the left, my anchor-man in Bangalore who was my liaison for vernacular programme production across Sri Lanka and India.

FEBA RADIO

David Dare
Programme Controller

After an exhausting period as Programme Controller, I returned to the UK and the Walton fellowship who had been so supportive throughout.

Comfort in bereavement

I was woken at 2 a.m. by loud banging and a distraught voice telling my host:

“**Your friend Raj has been found dead!**”

I was in Delhi and had met Raj (not to be confused with my anchorman in Bangalore) just hours earlier. He and other university students regularly enjoyed the warm hospitality and Bible studies of my Irish Missionary hosts.

These youngsters faced the same problems away from home as students worldwide. Here it including a particularly vicious drug scene in which Raj had become entangled. He had shown increasing interest in Jesus Christ but had remained involved with drugs and had now paid the price.

Two days later, an Uncle of Raj came to Delhi to investigate the circumstances of his nephew's death. At the University, he soon learned of the Missionaries' helpful friendship and he visited them to express his appreciation. I was there when he called.

The discussion was mutually sad and respectful. The Uncle did not take offence when he learned that his nephew had become interested in Jesus Christ even though his own religion was different.

After refreshments and pleasantries, the Uncle rose to leave. As he turned to say goodbye at the door, he spotted a poster on the opposite wall. It portrayed a large grave stone bearing the words of Jesus Christ:

"I am the resurrection and the life, he who believes in me will live even though he dies; and whoever lives and believes in me will never die." He stood silent for some seconds as we followed his gaze.

"Do you believe that?" he asked my host.

"Yes I do!" was the reply.

Then the Uncle asked, with some emotion, "Do you think that my nephew believed that?"

"I believe that he did." my host replied.

In a momentary gesture, which seemed to have special meaning, the Uncle was embraced by my host, and I knew that he had left with more than human comfort.

(Scripture Reference: John 11v25-26)

"A very poor gentleman"

Air India in the late 1970s managed to regularly lose my baggage, so I soon determined to travel with cabin luggage containing bare essentials in a shoulder bag and large briefcase. This included a small radio and cassette tape recorder and a change of clothes that I could wash and dry overnight. Indian travellers returning from overseas would arrive with everything but the kitchen sink, so two tall Sikh customs officials were surprised at my scanty possessions and enquired about the absence of my "shootcases". I assured them that I had none. As I walked away, I heard one exclaim, "He must be a very poor gentleman!"

Our Seychelles masts carried three huge 'curtain' aerials pointing roughly north-east, north and north-west. They would be activated according to when the sun rose over the target areas, first Sri Lanka and east India, then central and west India and later, Arabia and down east Africa. In this way, our programmes 'arrived' as people were awaking and going to work. This process reversed each evening. In the station broadcast studio, Seychellois staff followed a carefully prepared running order sheet. They loaded cassettes bearing the next programme, punctuated by cartridges bearing the appropriate announcement in whatever language was going on air at that moment. Library staff were responsible for lining up the cassettes and cartridges for the studio staff. The main responsibility of the studio staff, many with minimal, formal education was to keep exactly to the big clock on the studio wall in following the running order sheet. Generally, they were amazingly reliable and a pleasure to work with.

7. 1981-92: Return to UK; Marriage; Interior Decorating; Lloyds Life; Royal Life of Liverpool and Early Retirement

Rosemary Barnes (here with a friend) and I married soon after my return to the UK and I also began the adjustment back into secular life and searching for employment. I sent out ninety (90) applications, got nine interviews and then the Lord stepped in by way of David Collett, Seretary of Lloyds Life in London. More about that later!

John and Madge Langston got me into painting and decorating until I found employment with Lloyds Life, London

David Collett of Lloyds Life London who gave me the opportunity of re-entering secular employment after my years overseas.

The long office building at Peterborough resulted from two years of planning for the relocation of Lloyds Life from London

Here is my lovely cousin Doreen Beacham at Southend on Sea. She and her late husband Vic were hugely hospitable to my missionary family on visits during our years overseas and I was able to visit Doreen to thank her in October 2020.

Rosemary Barnes and I marry

While away from the UK, lovely Rosemary Barnes and I had maintained a steady friendship by post and she twice visited me in the Seychelles. On my return we were engaged and married. Her parents, who lived at Godalming, warmly welcomed me into their thoroughly Christian family as did twin brother Douglas and elder sisters Sheila and Brenda and their families. Sadly, Sheila has since passed away. Rosemary's father, Percy Barnes most generously paid for us to have two wedding receptions to accommodate the large number of loving families and other friends in the fellowship of the Walton-on-Thames Baptist Church fellowship.

Perhaps it was the change of temperature which brought on a bout of malaria immediately on my return. Great friends, ex Royal Navy Commander John and wife Kay Collingwood, cared for me through to my recovery and up to the wedding.

John had a dramatic experience near Hong Kong against the approaching Japanese air-force. His torpedo boat was refuelling at an offshore island. The crew were resting but his rear-gunner was sufficiently alert to sight a Japanese fighter aircraft approaching and shot it down as it attacked. Before that incident, the gunner had been a recalcitrant and troublesome member of John's crew and under warning. After this incident, John had grounds to better appreciate him.

Rosemary's parents, my new, loving in-laws, along with her twin brother Douglas (right) and wife Fiona brought great warmth into my life on my return to the UK.

Below – two couples who became hugely supportive in two of my Self-Employed assignments after early retirement from Royal Life of Liverpool.

Mr and Mrs Derek Wright of Peterborough Design Group supported me through assignments related to the Budget Insurance Offices and Estate refurbishment projects.

Mick and Lorraine Brookes of Financial Services Dot-Com with Rosemary.

Above are my precious parents among Salvation Army trainee Officers and (above right) a depiction of Jesus Christ whom they loved and served. It was mostly their inspiration and prayers that helped me to develop my own faith in Christ who I have found so faithful to me over the past fifty years.

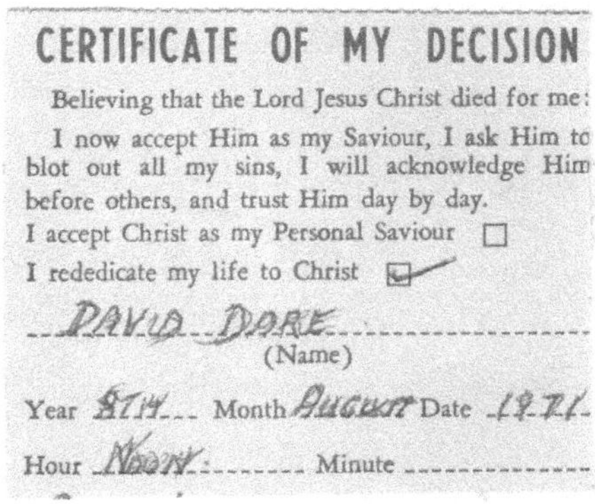

CERTIFICATE OF MY DECISION

Believing that the Lord Jesus Christ died for me:

I now accept Him as my Saviour, I ask Him to blot out all my sins, I will acknowledge Him before others, and trust Him day by day.

I accept Christ as my Personal Saviour ☐

I rededicate my life to Christ ☑

DAVID DARE
(Name)

Year 8TH Month AUGUST Date 1971

Hour NOON Minute

Finally, two families whose thoroughly wholesome parents were also an inspiration at just the right time.

Thank you Lord for them all.

The delightful Rabbiosi family of Mombasa

Sister Jessie and me with the The Phelps farming family of Arusha, Tanganyika (1940s)

Interior decorating

I introduce this subject with the name of John Langston. With seven years out of circulation, I had an unusual C.V. at the age of 42 with which to to apply for employment back in the UK. Finding a new career was to take a year during which church friend John Langston generously took me on, assisting his part-time decorating business. His ‘day job’ was in Air Traffic Control at Heathrow Airport.

During my first year back in the UK, I applied for ninety jobs and obtained eight unsuccessful interviews. Then, through a Weybridge employment agency, I was invited to visit Mr David Collett, the Christian company secretary of Lloyds Life in London, to be interviewed for their Office Services Manager vacancy. Someone better qualified got the job but only for two weeks. When the poor man was found to be an alcoholic, I was given the job which soon focussed on preparing that company for relocation to Peterborough two years later.

Lloyds Life of London and its relocation to Peterborough

Very shortly after joining Lloyds Life, they decided to escape the heavy overheads of central London and settled on developing a new office facility in Peterborough, Cambridgeshire. Working closely with Company Secretary David Collett who had employed me, I was heavily involved in preparing the move. About half of our 200 staff decided to move. We would replace the other half by recruiting local Peterborough staff ahead of the move.

We acquired a building under construction by the Peterborough Development Corporation and were involved in its extension to meet our needs. I was primarily charged with liaising with our department heads regarding the data, telecoms and furniture space planning and interior design and furnishings, all to be in place ready for re-commencement of business on the Monday morning after close of business in London the previous Friday evening.

Having arranged a moving contractor, all went well until their trucks stopped rolling on the Saturday. A new government regulation forced the drivers to take breaks. This had not been allowed for in our move. It seemed that we would not complete on time until I sent up an arrow prayer based on Romans 4v17: “Our God treats things that are not as if they are”. Based on that promise, I pleaded for help out of this impossible situation. Shortly, another crew of our contractor was turned away from a separate customer who defaulted and those trucks were re-directed to help complete our move. It was a close run thing but the result was pristine offices on the Monday and a handsome salary bonus for me.

Actually, this was the most complex business challenge of my life. I had been marvellously supported by Space Planning and Interior Design specialist Andrew Harding and subordinates in my own department. It was not to be long before Lloyds Life was purchased by Royal Life of Liverpool who had their own plans for our company. There hangs the following drama.

Royal Life of Liverpool

They decided that they needed to develop a UK-wide, Royal Liverpool computer centre to be based with us; that our building was too small and should be replaced by a monumental, new, climate efficient building on a virgin site which they had purchased in Peterborough. My remaining time with my now Royal employers was spent, uncomfortably, re-locating everyone once again to this new building. Again, I was ably assisted by my new Peterborough staff, Bernard Scotney – Admin, Brian Payne – engineering; Susan Beales – Space Planning, Peter Clifford – Maintenance, and my secretary Yvonne. The icing on the cake was when Royal offered me a most generous early retirement package and I found myself again unemployed aged 53.

8. 1993-2003: Final self employment

Oil distribution research, East Africa – my first, self employed assignment

I introduce this subject with the name of David Parsons. David was company secretary for a Greek family with oil shipping interests. They had a historical relationship with Uganda and were considering the possibility of bidding for that country's oil business. Before doing so, they asked me to examine the logistics of moving bulk supplies from the east African coast to the capital Kampala via two alternative means.

One was via the Kenya oil pipeline with the possibility of political disruption. The alternative was firstly by bulk tanker on the Tanzanian railway from Dar-es-Salaam on the coast to my birth place, Tabora – a trip of sentimental interest to me. Secondly, still by rail tanker, north to the Lake Victoria port of Mwanza. Thirdly, across the lake with the rail tankers loaded onto lake steamers to the north end of the lake at it's Entebbe port.

I discovered that a lack of rail maintenance of the first Dar to Tabora line was resulting in trucks regularly falling off the track. The Greek family dropped the idea of bidding.

In travelling that first leg, I had shared a two berth compartment with a local MP He had a sense of humour and said we would be approaching “The Hilton Hotel” stop for lunch. In fact we stopped at a minute station in the bush at midday where a market awaited us by our carriages. It was a time of drought and the locals were only able to offer us passengers the most meagre produce such as an egg, a glass of water, a cup of boiled rice, a banana. They were soon sold out as there was no catering on the train. I made my mark with the MP being able to share my stock of biscuits and coffee from my flask. He in turn opened up about the problems facing his son at University in Dar-es-Salaam. Apparently, pages were missing from the few books in its library.

When we arrived at Tabora, the MP’s large Toyota Land Cruiser and driver awaited him and he kindly saw me to the only African managed hotel in the town. I had chosen to stay there rather than the ‘more European’ Railway Hotel where my parents had stayed when they arrived in 1934. I was woken early the following morning by dear old, retired Salvation Army officer Amos Mnyampi, my father's first 1934 convert. He accompanied me to catch the 5.00am train to Mwanza.

In a complete digression, I move from the Tanzania railway to the Kenya line from Nairobi to Mombasa. I remember the game we played on the downward run to the coast about “Who would be the first to see the sea”. Now, a fascinating historical anecdote related to the building of that line around the year 1902:

A lost steam railway engine

Some twenty years after the line was completed, a retired engineer who had been involved in that contract was back in Kenya on holiday. He visited an Indian colleague from the time of the construction who was now station master some distance from the coast. While there, he went into the adjacent bush to hunt after game birds. He had just brought down a guinea-fowl in thick bush and realised in stooping to pick up a bird that he was standing between two rail lines. There, in front of him, stood a shunting steam locomotive. It was covered in undergrowth and isolated on short lengths of rail some distance from the main Mombasa/Nairobi line.

Armed with the engine's serial number, he returned to the nearest station where the staff all knew about the engine but had no idea how it came to be there. On visiting the Nairobi Railway Archives, he discovered an audit taken during construction of that railway which recorded the loss of a shunting engine. The visitor knew that activity up and down the line had been frantic and that many such engines were in use at the time. He also knew that spur lines were regularly constructed to temporary storage yards then removed as construction progressed.

He came to the conclusion that some engineer about to leave the country had instructed the labourers to remove this spur line which they must have done, ignoring an engine that was left stranded at the end of it. The "lost" engine now stands in the Nairobi railway museum but its power and usefulness was lost to the construction for the rest of the contract.

Like the staff at the station, it is possible to know that something is not quite right in life. It is also possible to not know why life feels incomplete. Saint Augustine said that we can go through life with a God shaped gap in us. We will not feel complete until we find Him.

The thing that most surprised me when I became a Christian was that God had always been close to me although I did not appreciate it. God, our Heavenly Father, tells us that his Son will never turn anyone away and promises to reside within our hearts as we trust in him.

(Scripture references: Matthew 17v5, John 6v37)

Budget Insurance and its estate – my second self employed assignment

I introduce this subject with two names – those of Les Blignaut of Budget Insurance and of Derek Wright of the Peterborough Design Group.

Les asked me to manage the refurbishment of a Peterborough estate and mansion purchased by their Managing director from the famous Perkins Diesel Engine family. My brief included provision of a sizeable lake for trout fishing and a sophisticated transformation of the mansion. Les and I agreed we needed to engage serious professional sub-contractors to cope. This is when Derek Wright and his Peterborough Design Company came in and saved the day through his limitless patience and architectural/engineering expertise and contacts.

The Air Freshener Company: my third self employed assignment

I introduce this subject with the name of Bill Yemps. Bill needed to relocate his head office and warehouse from Manchester to Stevenage and asked me to arrange it all. His product range included aerosol type tins for use in various public loos with mountings timed for periodic dispersal of the air-freshener aroma. Along the way, I stumbled across what seemed to be a looming and monumental oversupply of the tins for filling with their gas.

Ordering of components was not within my brief and I needed to be able to articulate my concern before it was too late. I went to the Peterborough library and after a little prayer, turned up a stock-flow equation. In applying that equation to the stock ordering position, it clearly proved that the company would incur huge over-expenditure in excess stock unless it immediately cancelled a shipment from the Far-East. Bill acted on this advice and – according to him this saved his job. My previous relocation experience helped me with the transfer of the warehousing which Bill described as "seamless". Derek Wright was again helpful with the interior design of the office facility.

Financial Services Dot Com: my fourth, self employed assignment

I introduce this subject with the name of Mick Brookes. Mick and I were attending the same church in Peterborough when he decided to climb onto the

DotCom bandwagon. Despite my complete lack of experience both in IT and the explosion of company start-ups, he asked me to join him. I was to assist with basic research in the expanding DotCom market and find us office space.

Jeff Lenton became the third member. He was about to wind up his IT business and had advertised his premises which I went to view. It was not suitable so we settled on an alternative. In the mean time, Jeff took an interest in our vision and joined us, generously donating his office I.T. equipment and furniture together with his experience and agreeable personality. We were then able to raise finance to grow the business which I left for retirement in 2003 having received my initiation in the basic use of the Personal Computer from these amenable and very patient colleagues.

9. 2003: Retirement to Lyme Regis

We retired to Lyme Regis in Dorset, from Peterborough, in 2003.

Prayer Partners

We soon found a spiritual home at the nearby Uplyme Church of England fellowship. Among new friends there, Terry and Sue Daly and Alan and Esther Jones shared our special interest in prayer. We would meet with the Dalys once a week at their Uplyme home, enjoy coffee and one of Sue's special biscuits and then we would get down to pray seriously about our common local or wider concerns.

Jack and Imogen Thomas were also an inspiration to us at this time.

Terry and Sue Daly

Alan and Esther Jones

These photos are especially precious to me because we lost Terry in 2010 and Alan passed away in 2020. Just before Terry's passing, he encouraged me to always remember Paul's letter to the Ephesians, chapter 3v18 about "grasping how wide and long and high and deep is the love of Christ." Similarly, Alan, who also loved Jesus, often had a word of encouragement from the Bible.

The Church of St Peter and St Paul at Uplyme

We have travelled frequently but home/garden, family, church and sports have given us a happy first seventeen years in Lyme Regis. Committed lay members have kept our church going during several changes of clergy.

Heroic staff at Uplyme village shop/post office and fuel station have been wonderfully supportive during the pandemic. Over these seventeen years, Dr Forbes Watson has expanded the Lyme Regis Medical Centre to cope with the health needs of a wider population.

Earthquake in New Zealand

Rosemary and I have enjoyed numerous holidays since retiring, especially at the Carmel Christian holiday farm at George, in the Western Cape, South Africa. Our most dramatic experience however, took place visiting New Zealand in 2011. We escaped injury during the 22nd February earthquake which killed 185 close to our hotel. We had only been there one night when it occurred and its severity is shown in this photograph (© asgq. "Christchurch earthquake damage" used under licence CC BY 2.0).

We rushed out of our hotel with just the clothes we had on and, fortunately, my wallet and diary with details of the two weeks ahead. Wonderfully, we were taken in by a local family (**more angels – Jurg and Shirley Honger and daughter Argene)** who set us on our way by helping us to hire a car the following day. The extraordinary factor which enabled them to do so was that when all telecoms and IT systems were disabled by the quake, our host "just happened" to have radio/telephone contact with his office which "just happened" to be located next to an Avis car hire depot. Avis generously provided us with a car with fuel in the tank when all Christchurch service station pumps were without electricity. Psalm 23v6 comes to mind about the "goodness and love of our Shepherd following us all the days of our lives".

Back in the UK and since retirement, we have been blessed in getting to know two lovely families and their holiday homes, the Rees family in Wales and the Nisbet family in Scotland. They have provided for most of our retirement breaks away from our pleasant Lyme Regis home where we are always on holiday!

Our angel on Gozo

During a short break to Gozo, an island adjacent to Malta, we were walking away from the main market down an empty, narrow, cobbled lane. I pulled my sunglasses out of my shirt pocket and without realising it, I must have dislodged our creditcard-sized hotel room key onto the ground as we walked along. Suddenly, an English accented voice behind us asked, "Is this yours sir?" It was a bright-faced lad with our key. I turned to Rosemary in surprise then immediately turned back to thank the boy who had disappeared. There was no sign of him back up the narrow lane.

Full circle and pause for reflection:

As a disciple of Jesus Christ, I have shared his Gospel through various means over the past near fifty years through FEBA radio broadcasts, pastoral visitations and door to door distribution of Gideon Bibles and literature. Response has been generally one of disinterest but the following, profound experience has encouraged me to joyfully entrust the end result to our Lord himself.

In Isaiah 55v11, God promises that HE does not allow any Gospel seeds we sow to 'return to Him empty' and Joel 2v28 promises "your old men will dream dreams". I had just such a dream directly related to sharing Christ's gospel.

In it I saw pentecostal type flames dotted among some hundreds of homes where I had deposited my 'Divine Comfort' leaflet during our first Covid-19 Lock-down. The leaflet carried a picture of Jesus calling the fishermen, and comforting verses from Psalm 91 plus John 3v16. Having previously put on the armour of God (Ephesians 6v10 etc.), I prayed for The Lord to bless the residents of each home with his peace and revelation of those scriptures. At each door, I sensed a spiritual conflict taking place with Satan – Revelation 12v9 – "who leads the whole world astray" blocking the minds of the recipients. I immediately related the flames I saw in the dream to the transformational power of the Holy Spirit – in this case, birthing in some of the residents a hope of eternal life through repentance and the gift of faith in Christ.

Through this experience, I have come to believe that God honours our obedience when we GO with his Gospel of Christ. As we sow seeds, God, as I understand it, reaps souls into his kingdom. We may only realise the results in eternity.

10. Postscript

It's time for me to end my tale but not before I thank the following people:

First and foremost my darling wife Rosemary who has been my loving companion and rock during our near forty years of marriage.

We are most grateful to Rosemary's sister Brenda and husband Brian for their local Lyme Regis hospitality and support, remembering too that it was Brenda who originally found our beautiful home for us above Lyme Bay.

We much appreciate the mutual encouragement we enjoy with my American nephew Barry Durman and his lovely wife Joanne (photo overpage).

Then there are the numerous, generous and loving folk whom I have omitted to mention.

Rosemary and I much appreciate Rob and Jo Smith for lovingly hosting our present home Bible Study group.

It has been a joy to renew contacts with the Beacham family and Salvation Army Fellowship at Southend-on-Sea where it all started.

At this point, I hesitate to mention the wonderful and gifted speakers and everyone else involved in the Uplyme church's services and other activities. I hesitate to do so because I am bound to miss somebody.

I am grateful to Ian and Caddy Dalton for their unstinting support in our Uplyme prayer ministry over the past five years. For me, this ministry has been the highlight of our membership of St Peter and St Paul's C of E fellowship at Uplyme near our home in Lyme Regis, Dorset.

We have held morning prayer meetings on four mornings each week since June 2015 until Covid lock-downs started in March 2020.

Latterly, we are encouraged by the suggestion from author Mathew Backholer that Intercessory Prayer can have three aspects: "1. Identification – to identify with a person or situation. 2. Agony – to agonise over a person or situation. 3. Authority – through listening to the Holy Spirit, one can learn the will of the Lord in the situation; and receive assurance that the matter about which one is praying will be answered in God's own way and time.

Here is a picture gallery of those who have participated in this prayer ministry:

Kay & Simon Kaffin-Johnson

Marilyn Kent (pictured with grand daughter Freya)

Ian & Caroline Doulton

Shirley Hobden

David Jones

Charles King

Simon Smith

Janet Impey

David & Rosemary Dare (shown with guest from Tanzania: Grace of the Salvation Army Mnyampi family mentioned earlier)

Dom Rogers

Andy Bateman

Graham Sheargold

Carol FOWKES

Kim Jeffrey

Ros Blackmoor

Mike Whittome

Brian and Brenda Stansfield and younger son Chris

I end this memoir with a prayer from an old hymn, on behalf of all who have encouraged me over these years: "Drop thy still dews of quietness, Till all our strivings cease; Take from our souls the strain and stress, And let our ordered lives confess The beauty of thy peace."

Au revoir

Lightning Source UK Ltd.
Milton Keynes UK
UKHW030847250321
380963UK00005BB/145

9 780992 75701